T0293090

Foundations
of Global Business

A Systems Approach

Foundations of Global Business

A Systems Approach

Nader H. Asgary

Bentley University

Dina Frutos-Bencze

Saint Anselm College

Massood V. Samii

Southern New Hampshire University

INFORMATION AGE PUBLISHING, INC.
Charlotte, NC • www.infoagepub.com

Library of Congress Cataloging-in-Publication Data

A CIP record for this book is available from the Library of Congress
http://www.loc.gov

ISBN: 978-1-68123-268-3 (Paperback)
          978-1-68123-269-0 (Hardcover)
          978-1-68123-270-6 (ebook)

Contents

SECTION I

The Institutional Structure of International Business

SECTION **II**

Firm Level International Business

List of Figures

Foundations of Global Business, pages xi–xii

Copyright © 2016 by Information Age Publishing

List of Tables

Foundations of Global Business, page xiii
Copyright © 2016 by Information Age Publishing

Acknowledgments

This book has been evolving from a more technical systems dynamic approach to the current form that focuses on thinking systematically about international business and therefore shall appeal to a broader audience. The initial methodology made it difficult for students and readers to appreciate the fundamental international business theories and concepts. Since we contributed equally to the development of the manuscript our names are listed alphabetically.

We would like to thank Dr. Pard Teekasap for his earlier contribution to the book as well as to Selina Marcille for reading the transcript and making editorial changes and corrections. In earlier stages, Aida Garcia compiled a number of chapters based on Dr. Samii's class lectures. We very much appreciate her efforts and contribution. Above all, we would like to acknowledge the contributions of our students who have made many constructive comments and suggestions to various drafts of the chapters.

Finally, we would also like to thank our families for supporting us during the writing and editing process. Dr. Nader Asgary is grateful to his family and especially his wife, Jila, for their unconditional support and encouragement. Dr. Frutos-Bencze would like to thank her family and especially Zsolt Bencze, for his encouragement. Dr. Samii would like to thank his wife Farideh Namazi Samii for support and encouragement throughout the process. She was instrumental and a motivational force for him in this project in particular and generally for his career.

Foundations of Global Business

A Systems Approach

Dynamics of Systems in Global Business

Global business is as old as business itself. Yet, in recent years international business has expanded considerably and has become very complex. New methods of doing business across borders, the variety and complexity of the steps involved in a business transaction, and the dynamic changes in the global business environment have created a new and complex environment for multinational enterprises (MNEs). In addition, organizations such as the World Trade Organization (WTO) that provide an institutional structure for trade, the emergence of information and communications technology (ICT), the integration of global financial markets, and the ease of travel overseas have created an environment that is both challenging and increasingly conducive to international business activities.

This book views international business as a complex and integrated system in its various dimensions. Particularly since those dimensions have changed considerably and most likely will continue to change in the future, we take a *systems approach* to study and analyze the changes because this is what is actually happening in the era of globalization.

Analysis of International Business: Systems Approach

The word system comes from the Greek systema or "organized whole, body," which in turn comes from *syn-* "together" and *histanai* "cause to

Foundations of Global Business, pages 1–11
Copyright © 2016 by Information Age Publishing
All rights of reproduction in any form reserved.

1

stand" and in its original acceptation meant "to cause to stand together" (Fowler & Fowler, 2011; Hoad, 1993). According to Senge et al. "a system is a perceived whole whose elements hang together because they continually affect each other over time and operate toward a common purpose" (Senge, 2006; P. Senge, Kleiner, Roberts, Ross, & Smith, 1994). On the other hand, Denis Sherwood defines a system as "a community of connected entities." His definition emphasizes the connectedness between the entities that comprise the system of interest (Sherwood, 2002).

Following a systems approach, we define *system* as the set of rules of operation and interaction, as well as the structure among various elements. Several smaller subsystems can be part of a larger system. Each can contain a number of subsystems that have a structure and logic of their own.

Elements that are outside the boundary of the system affect the elements of the system. At the same time, those external elements are affected by the system. There are several systems that are discussed in this book. For example, we consider global business to be a system that defines the way global business is done, as well as determines the rules of operation in the global business environment that MNEs follow.

The structure of global business has changed noticeably in the last two decades. Perhaps one of the most important new dimensions of the new global business order is the degree of integration across geographic boundaries, as well as across industrial sectors. No longer is the economic policy of a major country an isolated matter. Changes in the economic policy of China or the United States have repercussions on the policies of other countries through international trade and international finance.

The global economy can be viewed as an electric grid network in which nations are connected to each other through trade and investment. Using the network notation, each nation is a separate node that is connected to each other through a link. In an electric grid, if one of the small nodes runs into a problem, the rest of the system can adjust itself to prevent the collapse of the total system. But if one major node faces a problem, the system would not be able to handle the shortfall (or system overload) and the whole system would fail. The global economic system and business system are similar in the sense that countries outside the system are insulated from systemic risk, but on the other hand, they do not have the advantages and opportunities that the global system offers.

Systems thinking is an approach that considers the situation or a problem as a result of the structure of the system, not from an external event. In its broadest sense, systems thinking includes a large body of methods, tools, and principles that are oriented to look at the interrelatedness of forces and seeing them as part of a common process that shapes the system. System dynamics is one tool that approaches the problem or situation through the system perspective. Professor Jay Forrester and his colleagues at the Massachusetts Institute of Technology (MIT) initially developed system dynamics. The tools and methods that we use throughout the book are a system approach and are rooted in the understanding of how complex system structures generate patterns. In this case, we apply the tools and methods to all aspects of international business (Sterman, 2000).

Because system dynamics shows the interdependencies within a system, it does not focus on best policies. Rather, it tries to consider the impact of various policies and decisions on different variables in the system. The real challenge of the method lies in deciding among countless factors what to include and what to leave out when defining the system. In other words, the challenge is to define the system, set the boundaries, and understand the relationship between the various variables within the system.

The global economy has become a huge grid of trade, investment, and cultural exchange. More and more countries are recognizing the benefits of being part of the global network. International trade has increased dramatically in the last two decades with huge benefits to the participants by shifting resources where they receive the highest incremental productivity. This, in turn, has created employment and economic growth for countries with large labor forces and low wages, such as China and India. On the other hand, cheap input from low-wage countries has helped to keep importing costs and inflation down in the more developed and high-wage economies. It has also helped developed countries to shift their workforce to higher value added industries and to research and development. The dynamic aspect is also interesting. The growth in the national income of emerging economies will eventually translate to purchasing power and thus increase consumption that in turn will be an incentive for exports from developed economies to these emerging economies.

Global financial markets have also become increasingly integrated into a system. The global financial system has benefited investors in developed economies where the rate of return on investment has been fairly low. Investment flow to capital poor countries led to a higher rate of return for global investors. At the same time, capital poor countries that needed to attract funds from the global financial market benefited by receiving additional funds that fueled their economic growth. This resulted in a gain-gain situation. Indeed, the global financial market has become highly integrated.

The global economic and financial integration has also raised concerns for potential financial risk transferring among countries. International economic integration has not been without its drawbacks. There has been a great deal of concern about the loss of jobs from developed economies to emerging market economies. Multinational enterprises have shifted their investment overseas to enjoy cheap labor, thus creating concerns for unemployment in the developed economies.

The main dynamic vehicle in the evolution of global trade, investment, and commerce has been the firms. Enterprises, trading companies, financial firms, manufacturing and service enterprises, and logistic firms have all participated and played an active role in the evolution of the global system, and at the same time are impacted by the dynamic changes in that system. For example, Brazil, Russia, India, and China's (also known as the BRICs) move toward a market economy has led to the emergence of a great deal of opportunity for multinational enterprises. But at the same time, it has led to the emergence of large and competitive multinationals from these countries that have become formidable competitors for their Western counterparts. Emerging market multinationals such as China National Offshore Oil Corporation (CNOOC) or India's Wipro are becoming strong competitors and making the world competitive landscape increasingly more flat. Wipro, a Bangalore-based technology company, for example, has become a giant multinational operating in 70 countries and has revenue of more than $6 billion per year (Wipro, 2014).

Internal–External Systems

In this book, we look at international business as two separate systems: an external system, which is the system that includes all the aspects that are external to the firm such as the global environment in which the firm operates; and an internal system, which is the system that includes all the aspects related to a firm (the firm system).

In turn, the firm system consists of two subsystems. The first subsystem is the firm's functional subsystem that includes elements such as purchasing, production, operations, sales and marketing, and finance divisions. Depending on the size and complexity of a firm, the functional subsystem can have a number of subsystems. Alternatively, a firm can have a divisional subsystem. A large firm may have a number of different divisions that operate independently, but are interconnected strategically through resources and policies. All the international operation elements would be part of the firm's divisional subsystem.

The intangible assets of a firm, such as the management structure, research and development, and technology infrastructure encompass another firm subsystem. There are also less visible foundational aspects of a firm, such as its value system, leadership, policies, and corporate culture that would also be elements of this subsystem. These nested subsystems interact with each other and set the overall internal structure of the firm. These aspects are the foundation of the core competency of a firm and the basis for the strategy of the firm. The internal system is the key for formulations of firm strategy, while the external system provides the overall environment within which the strategy is formulated.

Additionally, we will discuss in detail each of these subsystems and their internal interaction, as well as their impact on the overall system. The book also discusses strategy formulation based on our systems framework.

Dynamic Elements of International Business

The external business environment, the internal resources, and the strategy of firms change over time. It would be misleading to assume that these elements remain static. Dynamic analysis focuses on the understanding of these changes and their impact. Factors that shape the overall political and economic environment of the international business environment are continuously changing. The international trade regime and the trade governing institutions have gone through a number of structural changes. The General Agreement on Tariffs and Trade (GATT) has become the World Trade Organization that as of 2010 included 161 members and observer countries.

Changes in the global business environment have created great opportunities, but at the same time they have created risks for multinational enterprises. The continuous change in the global marketplace is demanding that firms be more dynamic in all aspects of their enterprise's success. This has resulted in an overall increase in international trade and economic growth in the decade after establishment of the World Trade Organization. The increase in economic growth and international trade has created opportunities and challenges for multinational enterprises. It has led to additional resource requirements for expansion, but it has also led to the requirement of different resources to take advantage of new opportunities and to address the new risks. Such impacts call for the revision of current human resource policies and the creation of new policies and procedures to address and support the international strategy of a firm.

An important structural change has been the liberalization of the global financial market that has led to a greater integration across various markets. The openness of the global financial system brought a number of benefits to capital poor countries, including the transfer of capital from capital rich countries where the rate of return was low. This has helped poor countries supplement their capital structure and helped investors in rich countries gain higher rates of return. But there is also a dark side that has only become apparent over time. The global financial integration resulted in an increase of international systemic risk and led to risk transfer across the globe. As we saw, the financial meltdown of the United States in 2008 quickly spread to a number of other countries. The critical factor is the time path of changes from one country to another and from one industry to the next. In other words, the downturn of the financial market in the United States affected other countries and other industries over time.

Another example is the transition of the former centrally planned economies to a market economy. The impact of restructuring their economy was not felt right away on their domestic enterprises or on the firms abroad. The impact on opportunities and challenges for domestic and international firms in these transition economies only became clear after a number of years. Many large companies from emerging economies are becoming global competitors of the firms from developed economies. But at the same time, a great deal of partnerships have been developed between enterprises from emerging economies and developed economies that benefit both sides.

A systems approach allows us to see the impact of the internal functional and foundational aspects of the firm from a dynamic viewpoint. For example, many firms enter into an international partnership for different reasons, including improvement in their earnings, increasing their market share, gaining competitive advantage, reducing costs, and diversifying risk. Another advantage of an international partnership is learning from a partner. These knowledge advantages are in the form of learning a new technology, operational efficiency, and learning about the local competitive environment. Learning benefits will only materialize over a period of time. Focusing on static benefits and costs will fail to spot a major long-term advantage of an international partnership.

The following factors introduce dynamic elements in the external global business environment:

1. Government policies including regulations in various countries (i.e., privatization, nationalization or a tariff change)
2. Political and commercial relationships between various countries (i.e., relations between the United States and China)
3. Global institutional structure (World Trade Organization, or WTO, shift to floating exchange rate)
4. Cultural attitude (cultural convergence)

5. Industry life cycle (maturing product structure and moving abroad, product life cycle theory)
6. Interindustry competitive structure (foreign firm entry into the domestic market, U.S. auto industry.)

These issues will be discussed in detail in subsequent chapters.

System Dynamics Language

System dynamics (SD) is a methodology that is used for the analysis of dynamic paths of various variables in a complex system through a systems approach. System dynamics enables us to observe the change of a complex situation such as globalization in a systems manner. In other words, it allows us to view the complex situation as a network of causes and effects of all the factors that are related to the particular situation. System dynamics can also simulate the behavior of the system over time using differential equations and calculus. In this book, we primarily focus on using models to show relationships to conceptually understand the impact of changing one variable or element on the system as a whole. However, we also provide specific examples and cases where mathematical models are included.

Causal Loop Diagrams

To better understand the structure of a system and the behavior pattern such a system will generate, we use the system dynamics notation for representing system structures. From any element or variable in a situation or system, arrows and links can be traced to represent the causal relationship of one variable on another element or variable. The diagram created shows the relationships between the variables that are difficult to describe verbally because normal language presents interrelations in linear cause-effect chains, while the diagram shows that there are feedback chains of cause and effect (Morecroft, 2007; Sherwood, 2002; Sterman, 2000). The influence of a variable can have a positive or a negative influence on another element or variable, and a curved arrow commonly represents it.

While at its core the approach of this book is based on system dynamics, we do not use causal loops and the technical language of system dynamics to explain the topics that are discussed.

In the past three decades, significant economic, political, and cultural changes have made international business more exciting, complex, and challenging. Trade barriers have continuously been lowered and the revolution in technology and communications have facilitated and enhanced cooperation among countries, firms, and citizens of the world. This has created opportunities for great expansions in international business and has relatively flattened the playing field for small and medium size companies by allowing them access to global markets. The continuous emergence of new economies in the global competitive and commercial markets, especially the development of the economies of China, Eastern Europe, India, Russia, and Brazil, as well as many others, has created opportunities for international business activities but has also created potentially formidable competitors. Nongovernmental organizations (NGOs) have progressed in addressing some issues, such as poverty, the environment, human rights, and corruption. However, significant progress in these areas is required. Additionally, multinational enterprises (MNEs) from emerging economies have also impacted international business. The exponential growth in international business has brought new challenges for economic efficiency and has new applications emerging, such as the system dynamics approach. Firms that conduct international business are faced with many internal and external challenges that cannot be thoroughly analyzed with traditional tools.

This book presents the fundamentals of the international business environment, international business strategy, and international management. The text describes the various political, economic, and sociocultural environments that are critical for the successful operation of MNEs. Any firm keen to operate internationally needs to understand and be able to apply the institutional frameworks presented in this book. In addition, firm-level strategies for international operations are discussed in detail. Other fundamental topics such as global integration, leadership, and corporate social responsibility are discussed as well.

This approach enables readers to learn global business opportunities and risks in a comprehensive and integral manner. The topics presented in this condensed way allow practitioners, scholars, and students of international business to have a broad understanding of the most relevant issues in a changing international environment.

Many books in the field of international business, global strategy, and international management extensively address important aspects of international business. This book is original and unique in that it unites and links external and internal factors affecting international businesses.

We believe this book will be especially welcomed by faculty and students because of its succinctness and the up-to-date readings and case study recommendations. The book can be used in undergraduate and MBA courses such as international business, global strategy, international management, and strategic management since it would be more applied and less technical.

Chapter Descriptions

This book is composed of two sections. Section 1 discusses globalization, the political economy, the international trade system, and the institutional structure of international business. Section 2 addresses strategy, cross-cultural management and corporate social responsibility. Therefore, the book presents macro and micro level content in a cohesive and logical manner.

Section I: The Institutional Structure of International Business

Chapter 1: Globalization and Political-Economic Transformation

In this chapter we discuss the concept of globalization and its political-economic implications. Topics such as economic structures and institutional, nongovernmental organizations along with challenges for our generation are analyzed.

Chapter 2: The Global System

In this chapter, we define the global system as a structure of international order that consists of international political, economic, and sociocultural systems. These systems explain the relationships between nations and across geographical boundaries, and even the relationships within a country and among the different income groups, as well as among the modern and traditional sectors of a country.

Chapter 3 : The International Trade System

In this chapter the structure of the international trading system is discussed. Also, the concept of free trade and its implications and the main theories of international trade are covered. International trade theorists have developed several frameworks for policy analysis, and evaluation of the impact of trade on the participants and the dynamic shift in competitive advantage are presented as well.

Chapter 4: Economic Integration

As regional trade agreements and arrangements have increased over the past three decades, determining the precise cause of their proliferation and their effects has been a challenge for economists on intellectual and policy levels. The aim of the chapter is to understand the forces that drive economic integration, become familiar with the major existing trade agreements, understand the benefits and disadvantages of economic integration, and finally understand the effects of economic integration on foreign direct investment.

Chapter 5: The Global Financial System

The global financial system is defined by two components: global financial institutions and global financial markets. Global financial institutions include the International Monetary Fund (IMF), regional financial institutions, the World Bank, and regional development banks. The main function of these institutions is to help in the economic development of their members and to stabilize the financial and economic environment. The goal of this chapter is to understand the structure of the global financial system and become familiar with the institutions involved, also the functioning of currency markets and the factors that impact the exchange rate structure are explained.

Section II: Firm Level International Business

Chapter 6: International Business Strategy

Strategy is a roadmap for the future of an organization. It provides guidance for various stakeholders including investors, management, and other people working in the organization. This chapter explains the process of strategic planning and the relationship between the international and the overall business strategy of a firm. In addition, various aspects of international business strategy and models, such as the tripod model and its applications, are discussed.

Chapter 7: Location Selection

Companies internationalize for different reasons and finding the best location to expand a firm is crucial. The chapter discusses the process of selecting an optimal location to establish a business as well as the important factors that need to be considered when making location selection decisions.

Chapter 8: The Internationalization Process of a Firm

International business and commerce provide a great potential for value creation. Although there is no agreement on the definition of internationalization, there are several internationalization theories that try to explain why there are international activities. This chapter discusses the process of internationalization and explores the different options firms have.

Chapter 9: Cross-Cultural Management

Global managers need to have a mindset that enables them to clearly link end users' interests with the company's strategic goals and objectives. This means a manager has to engage cross-cultural employees in the success of the company skillfully and ethically, in addition to efficiently building an organizational structure that is capable of delivering the best output possible. This chapter reviews the fundamental issues of how a global manager can be interculturally effective in managing change in a global organization.

Chapter 10: Corporate Social Responsibility and Environmental Sustainability

Corporate social responsibility (CSR) and environmental sustainability are at the forefront of strategic and managerial agendas. Understanding these concepts is crucial for the implementation of any CSR and sustainability framework that will not only enhance a firm's performance, but also ensure future productivity and success.

SECTION I

The Institutional Structure of International Business

1

Globalization and Political-Economic Transformation

The objective of this chapter is to explain the concept of globalization, its driving factors, and implications. In this process we will become acquainted with the global political and economic structures and organizations involved in globalization. Additionally, we will present the advantages and disadvantages of globalization for host and home countries. Furthermore, we will evaluate the link between globalization and the bottom of the pyramid challenges and opportunities.

The renowned economist and Nobel Prize winner Joseph Stiglitz defines globalization as follows:

> Globalization is the closer integration of the countries and peoples of the world...brought about by the enormous reduction of costs of transportation and communication, and the breaking down of artificial barriers to the flows of goods, services, capital, knowledge, and people across borders. [He also states that] Globalization encompasses many things: the international

Foundations of Global Business, pages 15–23
Copyright © 2016 by Information Age Publishing
All rights of reproduction in any form reserved.

flow of ideas and knowledge, the sharing of cultures, global civil society, and global environmental movement. (Stiglitz, 2007)

Dani Rodrik, also a renowned political economist, has stated that the natural benchmark of globalization is to consider a world in which the markets for goods, services, and factors of production are perfectly integrated. His conclusion is that we are far from being fully integrated given the uneven playing field within and across countries in terms of economic opportunities and conditions (Rodrik, 2008).

Besides knowing the definition of globalization, it is also important to understand globalization's driving factors and implications. A certain level of convergence of economic, cultural, political, and social aspects is currently observable. Another aspect that must be addressed is whether global governance is required for sustainable globalization. The emergence of the G20, the group of 20 finance ministers and central bank governors from 20 major economies that collectively comprise more than 80% of the world's GDP, is a step forward toward inclusivity for finding common ground and convergence.

There are several driving factors that have helped the globalization process. The developments in communications and transportation technology have helped to reduce overall costs and improve communications. The Internet, teleconferencing, email systems, and texting are examples of technological innovations in communications. These innovations enable us to know about products or services created in other regions and facilitate the exploration of new markets.

Another driving factor of globalization is trade liberalization. Many countries have been reducing their barriers to trade and investment in order to take advantage and benefit from globalization. Economic liberalization is perceived by many as beneficial for the economy in the long run since it enables the entrance of new products and services in the market at lower prices, which in turn increases domestic competition. Serious attempts toward privatization and change in policies by a large number of developing countries to attract private investment have also helped the expansion of global investment and the flow of funds across borders. Thus, cross border flow has been beneficial for Greenfield investment as well as mergers and acquisitions.

The liberalization of the global financial system has led to further integration and convergence of financial performance standards for multinational enterprises (MNEs). This aspect has also been an important dimension of globalization. In addition, another outcome of global financial integration has been the need for rethinking corporate governances across borders.

The rapid and dynamic transformation of the economic landscape across the globe has had a significant impact on cultural, social, and political matters within and among countries. Globalization, which started with the concept of efficient allocation of economic resources by reducing and eliminating barriers to trade and investment, has led to various economic opportunities and created some challenges for business, governments, and people.

The reduction and elimination of barriers to the movement of capital, goods, services, and, in some instances, labor (e.g., in the European Union) have provided opportunities for businesses to establish themselves throughout the world. MNEs are taking advantage of lower cost labor and expanding consumer markets.

Economic growth and overall global prosperity have been noticeable in the last two decades. There has been considerable debate about the benefits and costs of globalization. Notwithstanding the debate, the process has been moving forward and, by all indications, will continue in the foreseeable future.

Debate on Globalization

Among the most debated and controversial issues regarding international economics and international business has been the impact of globalization on the economies of host countries and home countries. The proponents of globalization argue that international trade and investment have been instrumental in the economic growth of host countries where investment is flowing from home countries. Opponents argue that there have been considerable drawbacks both economically and socioculturally for the host countries. The list below summarizes the pros and cons of globalization based on the host and home country relationship.

Pros

- **Economic growth:** Incentivizes economic growth of developing economies (host countries). Therefore, it will improve the purchasing power of developing economies.
- **Higher employment:** Creates employment through export and foreign direct investment in both developing and developed economies (host and home countries).
- **Cheaper products:** Provides lower cost products for developed economies (home countries).
- **Innovation:** Globalization is also believed to stimulate innovation.

- **Global marketplace:** Globalization leads MNEs to consider distant countries as places for producing or for looking for suppliers. The process is leading to the creation of one global marketplace.

Cons

- **Employment loss:** The movement of jobs overseas may result in the loss of employment in developed countries and consequently prevent wage and salary increases. On the other hand, employment losses can also occur in developing countries when MNEs seek particular skills and increased domestic competition.
- **Competitive pressure:** In the developing countries, the concern is that large multinationals may lead to increased competitive pressure on the local companies that are smaller and do not have enough resources to compete. For instance, it would be difficult for smaller national retail stores to compete with Walmart in developing countries.
- **Loss of sovereignty:** The existence of international trade agreements will diminish countries' sovereignty and freedom from external control by curtailing their ability to act in their own best interests. Small countries are particularly concerned that their dependence on a larger country for supplies and sales will make them vulnerable to the demands of a country they might oppose.
- **MNE political interference:** Large international companies may be so powerful that they can dictate the terms of their operations by getting involved in local politics.
- **Convergence:** Globalization brings convergence of work methods, social structures, and even language, which might threaten local sociocultural characteristics and traditions.
- **Environmental risk:** Many developing countries do not have strict environmental laws and enforcement mechanisms. Therefore, the concern is that multinationals would move polluting industries into the countries that either don't have environmental regulations or that are not enforcing those laws.
- **Growing income inequality:** While developing countries benefit from economic growth, the benefits are not distributed evenly. The global trend is that rich people are becoming richer and poor people are becoming poorer. In other words, the gap between rich and poor is widening.

Globalization and Institutional Factors

Lin and Nugent defined an institution as a set of humanly devised be-havioral rules that govern and shape the interaction of human beings by partially helping them to form expectations of what other people will do (Lin & Nugent, 1995). An institution provides several elements: formal and informal rules of behavior, means of enforcing rules, conflict resolu-tion, and supporting market transactions. Rodrik states that institutions can create or destroy incentives for individuals to engage in trade, invest in human and physical capital, and encourage innovation. Thus, institutions have always played an essential role in governmental regulation and busi-ness operations; however, their role has become more relevant since the advent of globalization.

Technological developments have not only allowed for faster and easier transportation, communication, and trade between nations, but they have also led to the development of relevant institutions (WTO, 2004a). This has influenced governments to provide more effective governance and ser-vices than before. For example, European nongovernmental organizations (NGOs) have a greater influence than NGOs of other developed countries (Calame, 2008).

The political dimension of globalization is also an important one and it can be viewed from two different perspectives: first the impact and the role of multinationals on the political process of host and home countries, and second is the issue of the influence of the political structure of the country on the global business structure. In this context, corruption in internation-al business activities has received considerable attention in recent years.

The political system and environment of a country affect all the com-panies and their ways of doing business. The political impact is higher for international companies, since their presence in several countries means they are subjected to different political systems. It has been demonstrated that only international companies that accept and try to adapt to different political systems are the ones that will succeed. On the other hand, many multinationals have an income that far exceeds the gross national income (GNI) of some of the developing countries in which they operate. These multinationals could potentially influence the internal political-economic process of the country in which they operate.

The role that governments and institutions of civil societies play is es-sential for the development of a country. Globalization has transformed the role of government in two ways: (1) the traditional role of all players has been strained; and (2) the capacity of governments and their nongovernmental partners to deliver high quality public services has been challenged (Kettl, 2000).

Nongovernmental Organizations (NGOs)

Globalization has led to the empowerment of nonstate actors such as multinational corporations, nongovernmental organizations, international organizations such as the World Trade Organization (WTO) and the United Nations (UN), which will be discussed later, and transnational activist networks. States remain the primary actors for handling social and political externalities created by globalization. Powerful states use a range of foreign policy substitutes to advance their preferences into their desired outcomes. Nonstate actors can still influence outcomes on the margins, but their interactions with the states are more nuanced than the globalization literature suggests. Globalization undercuts state sovereignty, weakening governments' ability to effectively regulate their domestic affairs (Drezner, 2001).

Rising pressure and the desire of citizens of developing countries to attain the quality and living standards of developed nations, supported by globalization forces, have forced a major transformation in most developing governments. There are cases in which institutions and other nonstate actors have filled the governance void. In developed countries, institutions and private organizations are integrated into society, while in developing countries they are still evolving. The role of nationally representative and globally responsive governments is crucial in addressing today's discourse in the global arena. Also modifying the current management of international organizations such as the International Monetary Fund (IMF) and the World Bank is essential for sustainable development in a globalized world. The type of globalization that should be embraced is the one that can economically empower the greatest number of people and that is also socially and environmentally responsible.

As a result, many governments have to consider the influence and power of nonstate actors in decision making. Globalization has caused national governments to think and act globally. However, there are those who argue that this process has undermined the ability of some governments to continue to act as they used to.

The impact of nonstate actors can be seen across the developing and developed world. The National Intelligence Council (NIC-Eurasia) Group categorizes the political structure of nations as weak modernizing, and developed/post-industrial (NIC, 2014). Nations can be categorized according to the impact of nonstate actors in three general categories:

1. Developing
2. Transitional
3. Developed

In general, nonstate actors have had more freedom in developing and developed nations than in transitional ones. Many of the developing nations tend to be former colonies where governments struggle to provide order (i.e., Afghanistan, Somalia, Lebanon, Congo, and others). In this group, different nonstate actors may seriously challenge the central government and may be a substitute for governments in providing services. For example, in some African countries, the World Health Organization (WHO) has played an important role in alleviating HIV and the Ebola pandemics, with different levels of success in different countries.

Transitional states are sovereign nations that are in transition from a centrally planned economy to a market economy. In countries where the national government was strongly involved in managing the affairs of the nation, such involvement has now been diminished. These countries view foreign nonstate actors as a nuisance to national sovereignty and may attempt to influence and regulate their operation. For example, a number of countries have attempted to oppose pressure from human rights organizations. Another example is the pressure to provide intellectual property rights protections.

In developed countries where institutional structures are well developed, the nonstate actors tend to focus on challenging violations of ethical standards by governments and multinational corporations. For example, the recent movement Occupy Wall Street is against abuses of unregulated financial markets.

Table 1.1 summarizes the role of nonstate actors and their perception.

TABLE 1.1 Non-State Actors' Roles and Perceptions

Nation	Institutional Structure	Nonstate Actors	Role of Nonstate Actors
Developing	Ineffective	Economic: Free to operate Political: restricted	Economic: Supportive of government Political: Threatening government
Transitional	Taking shape	Economic: Some restricted operation Political: Some are restricted	Economic: Challenging to government Political: Challenging to government
Developed	Effective	Free to operate	Economic: Challenging to government Political: Challenging to government

Scholars, such as Dani Rodrik and Joseph Stiglitz, argue that in order to be more internationalized, voters and citizens need to start thinking globally rather than locally (Rodrik, 2008). However, when local services are not provided, citizens tend to reject the idea of globalization. What will the government's influence be in this post globalization world? Is the current globalization model sustainable? Are there models where institutions and governments work well together and help each other develop? These are all timely questions that need to be addressed.

Challenges of Our Generation

The current state of the world shows significant economic disparity among citizens worldwide. Additionally, the degree of citizen participation in formulating political systems varies dramatically among countries. There are many democratic systems of government in the world and there has been an exponential growth in the number of democratic governments since World War I. There are many nondemocratic governments with limited citizen participation and therefore, viable economic, political, and social institutions have not yet developed. Sustainable globalization requires addressing existing economic and political disparities. Jeffrey Sachs states that:

> To be able to advance the Enlightenment vision of Jefferson, Smith, Kant, and Condorcet our generation's work can be defined in the Enlightenment terms:
> - To help foster political systems that promote human well-being based on the consent of the governed
> - To help foster economic systems that spread the benefits of science, technology to everyone in the world
> - To help foster international cooperation in order to secure a perpetual peace
> - To help promote science and technology in human rationality to improve the human condition. (Sachs, 2006a)

His main message is to improve human well-being in a socially and environmentally conducive manner.

The Base of the Pyramid (BoP) concept was introduced by C. K. Prahalad. The main argument is that the BoP consists of approximately 5 billion people with an income of less than $2 per day who constitute a market that cannot and should not be overlooked (Prahalad, 2009).

The Base of the Pyramid has the following characteristics (London & Hart, 2010):

■ Heterogeneous across multiple dimensions

- Includes the portion of the world's population with the least amount of income.
- Contains local enterprises that generally are well integrated with the formal capitalist economy
- Constitutes the majority of humanity
- Exists primarily in the informal economy

This base can be both a market for products as well as a source of inexpensive input factors. The BoP does not have access to world class products or services, nor to the world market. It does not have experience in marketing, modern business processes and management, or financial resources either. In other words, the global knowledge of the BoP is limited. However, at the same time, the BoP provides both opportunities and challenges for MNEs in terms of value creation. The BoP not only provides the MNEs with low-cost labor, but it also creates a potential market for MNEs' products. Investment and job creation will lead to increases in the per capita income of the BoP that in turn will lead to increases in their purchasing power and consumption. While initially it is possible to make a fortune from the BoP, the opportunity increases drastically and exponentially over time.

2

The Global System

In this chapter, the concept of a global system is presented. Current political and economic systems are described as well as the relationship between these two systems and sociocultural systems that also have an impact. Additionally we will discuss its implications of new trends for the global system.

We define the global system as a structure of international order that consists of the international political, economic, and sociocultural systems. These systems explain the relationships between nations, and even the relationships within a country and the different income groups and economic sectors of a country.

Recently, these systems have evolved in major ways. Dynamic factors such as information and communications technology and international organizations have been the driving forces behind the changes in the global economic, political, and sociocultural systems.

Figure 2.1 illustrates the interrelation between these systems. Each system is discussed in detailed later in the chapter.

Foundations of Global Business, pages 25–33
Copyright © 2016 by Information Age Publishing

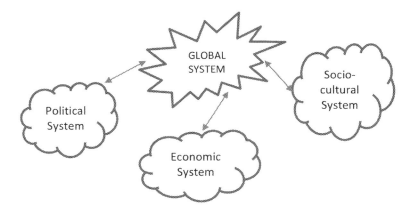

Figure 2.1 Global system and its components.

Multinational enterprises (MNEs) have also played a key role in shaping global business and the economic system. They are intermediaries in transferring products through trade, foreign investment, and technology. MNEs have been both praised and criticized for their role in shaping the global system. They have been praised for being instrumental in the economic transformation of many less developed countries to vibrant and growing economies. At the same, time they are criticized for focusing too much on short-term value maximization of their businesses at the expense of both their home country and the host country. There have been cases in which MNEs' treatment of the local workforce and compliance with environmental regulations have been considered to violate ethical principles. For example, the Blood Diamond case and trial of Charles Taylor, the former Liberian president, is a good example. Another example is the unethical operation of Shell Corporation in Africa in terms of environmental issues.

The Political System

Fundamentally there are two main political systems: democratic and non-democratic. In a democratic system leaders are elected by a majority vote, by consensus, or by direct referendum. The elected representatives of the people in turn are responsible for those who have elected them. Even though there is no specific, universally accepted definition of democracy, equality and freedom have been identified as important characteristics of democracy since ancient times.

In a democratic system there are periodic elections. Therefore, the political leaders and the party they represent must be responsive to the needs of their constituencies. In this system, economic and policy issues are debated and the pros and cons are articulated not only for the leadership's decision-making process, but also for the voting population.

In a nondemocratic system, which is a totalitarian system or a dictatorship, the leadership does not change by election or popular vote. Instead the leaders are in power through inheritance or by force. In either case, the decision flow is from top to bottom. In this system, the view and interest of the ruler or dictator is important, but the view of the population is not necessarily relevant. Usually, in totalitarian regimes changes are abrupt and possibly violent when a group seeks to overthrow the leadership.

Which system is more conducive to economic growth? There are those who claim that a democratic system is slow in terms of decision making since all decisions need to be debated and agreed upon. Therefore the process can be time consuming and slow. In a totalitarian system decision making is faster. But the problem with a totalitarian system is that the interests of the dictator (or the ruling group) may not reflect the interests of the majority of the people. Rather, in most cases, the objective of dictators is to serve themselves and their allies at the expense of the population. Moreover, in a dictatorship, policy issues are not debated, therefore the cost versus benefit of policies is not apparent to the population.

The Economic System

Economic systems also have two variants: a market economy and a centrally planned economy. In a market economy, major economic decisions are made by the market. In a centrally planned economy, the planning authorities make major economic decisions. Nowadays, it is difficult to find a purely centrally planned economy or a purely market economy. Most countries have elements of both.

What are the main economic decisions? The main economic decisions are the allocation of resources such as capital, labor, natural resources, and products to be produced. In a pure market economy, economic decisions are made by the market through a price mechanism. For example, how much of each good is to be produced depends on their relative price ratios and the cost of production, which takes into account the wage structure within each particular industry. Investment allocation in a market economy depends on the rate of return on investment and the profit within each industry. At the firm level, competitive performance would determine the success and future growth of the firm. In contrast, in a centrally planned economy the government planners make all those decisions.

Each system has some drawbacks. In a centrally planned system, re-source allocation could be suboptimal since the decision makers have no way of knowing whether or not their decision was the best one. In the absence of a price mechanism, making the optimal decision among many different choices would be difficult if not impossible. In a more technical sense, the preferences of the decision maker(s) may not correspond to that of the society as a whole.

The communist system used central planning as the core of its economic management. In a communist system, the ownership of production factors belonged to the government. There was limited private ownership and the private sector did not play a major role in the economy. Some small services were permitted to have private ownership, but major services, manufacturing, infrastructure, and social services all were owned and managed by the government.

The market economy also has issues and it is far from being a perfect system. An unregulated market economy may lead to the concentration of assets and economic power in the hands of a small group that could abuse this power. In addition, there is the potential for moral hazard so that some may abuse their economic position and continuously exploit others for profit (Krugman & Wells, 2012). In economic theory, moral hazard is a situation in which a party insulated from risk behaves differently from how it would behave if it were fully exposed to the risk. Moral hazard arises because an individual or institution does not take the full consequences and responsibilities of its actions, and therefore has a tendency to act less carefully than it otherwise would, leaving another party to hold some responsibility for the consequences of those actions. Also, market economies go through cycles of expansion and contraction called business cycles. The social cost of a business cycle in terms of both financial losses for firms and human suffering during a contraction period is considerable (e.g., the U.S. real estate bubble). Therefore, in a market economy, policies and regulations that prevent the abuse of economic power are needed, and financial safety nets that protect individual citizens in contracting economic cycles are essential.

The interaction of the economic system and political system is interesting (see Figure 2.2). In most cases political authoritarianism goes hand in hand with centrally planned economies. Also, market economies are most often found in democratic countries. While this is the norm, there are cases where a totalitarian society has a highly market driven economy, or that a number of democracies have a socialist economic system. Many of the Persian Gulf countries such as the United Arab Emirates (UAE), Qatar, and Bahrain have market economies, but the political systems are totalitarian

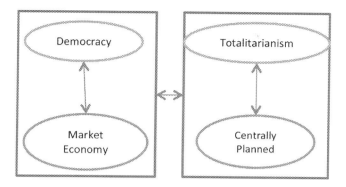

Figure 2.2 Connection between political and economic systems.

ones. In Europe, social democratic parties play an important role and have been in power for decades.

A socialist economic system is a structure that is somewhere in between a full market economy and a full centrally planned economy. In a socialist system, a number of major social functions such as health care and education are the responsibility of the government. The government also develops the country's infrastructure such as roads, airports, electric power system, water resources, telecommunication, etc. However, private firms have the possibility of participating in many different manufacturing and service industries. In a socialist system, the financial resources for government investments have to come from taxes. Therefore in socialist countries, the marginal tax rate is quite high. Since some of the government-owned firms get subsidies from the public sector, there is less emphasis on profitability and efficient use of resources.

Transition Economies

The major centrally planned economy was the communist regime of the former Soviet Union (Union of Soviet Socialist Republics) that consisted of 15 republics. Although the Soviet Union was technically a union of republics, the economy was centralized and had a single-party political system dominated by the Communist Party until 1990. Countries such as Poland, Czech Republic, Slovakia, Hungary, Romania and Bulgaria, also known as satellite countries, were formally independent from the Soviet Union, but were under heavy political and economic influence and control by the Soviet Union.

During the 1980s, the economic pressure was building on the Soviet Union making it difficult to support the various republics and satellite countries of Central Asia and Eastern Europe. As the Soviet Union's control of its satellite countries weakened, these countries began restructuring their economic and political system toward a market economy and a democratic political system in the early 1990s. The transition of the East European economies to market economies became a reinforcing cycle that started with East Germany's unification with West Germany and continued with the dissolution of the former Soviet satellite countries that joined in the reform process. In addition, many of the Central Asian Soviet republics became independent states from Russia and began the process of transition to market-based economies. Russia also began restructuring its economy.

The process of transition from a centrally planned to a market-based economy was not limited to the breakup of the Soviet Union. China, the most populated centrally planned economy, also started a transition toward a market economy in the late 1970s. Although China still has a communist political regime, it has slowly begun the economic transition by loosening government control of the economy.

Countries such as Brazil and India did not have a communist political system, but had strong government control of the economy, particularly through import substitution policies and restrictive foreign investment policies. These countries also began an economic change toward a market-based system. All the countries that start the process of restructuring their economic system toward a market-based economy are called transition economies.

In order to make a successful transition from a centrally planned economy to a market-based economy, many other conditions must be present. The International Monetary Fund (IMF) has defined those conditions for a successful transition as follows:

1. Liberalization: The process of allowing most prices to be determined in free markets and lowering trade barriers that had shut off contact with the price structure of the world's market economies.
2. Macroeconomic stabilization: Primarily the process through which inflation is brought under control and lowered over time after the initial burst of high inflation that follows liberalization and the release of pent-up demand. This process requires discipline over the government budget and the growth of money and credit (that is, discipline in the fiscal and monetary policy) and progress toward sustainable balance of payments.
3. Restructuring and privatization: The processes of creating a viable financial sector and reforming the enterprises in these

economies to render them capable of producing goods that could be sold in free markets and of transferring their ownership into private hands.

4. Legal and institutional reforms: The process of redefining the role of the state in these economies, establish the rule of law, and introduce appropriate competition policies. (IMF, 2000)

Emerging economies have become an important part of the global system. Four of the emerging economies Brazil, Russia, India, and China (called BRIC countries) collectively have a population of more than 2.6 billion and have an economic growth far exceeding that of the United States and Europe. Integration of these countries into the global economic system has created a major change in the global economy. It has created a large pool of low-cost labor in China and India, and it has opened a large market with increasing purchasing power. But at the same time, it has also created an increasing demand on the use of natural resources and on the environment. At the firm level, the restructuring of the global economic system discussed above has created a number of large multinationals from these emerging economies that have become competitors of U.S. and European multinationals.

Sociocultural System

In 2002, the United Nations Educational, Scientific and Cultural Organization (UNESCO) defined culture as follows:

> Culture should be regarded as the set of distinctive spiritual, material, intellectual and emotional features of society or a social group, and that it encompasses, in addition to art and literature, lifestyles, ways of living together, value systems, traditions and beliefs. (UNESCO, 2002)

These differences in how people interact with each other can cause several challenges in cross-cultural business relations. Cultural differences are an important barrier when doing business in the world. Other factors such as the legal system, access to information, and the language barrier have also been identified as critical challenges. It may be uncomfortable to interact with a businessperson of a different culture for the very first time. One might not know how to begin a conversation, how to greet the other person, how to negotiate with the other culture, or how to interact socially with them.

Individuals can be categorized according to their cultural perspectives as follows:

Ethnocentric: Individuals judge others by their own cultures.
Polycentric: Individuals easily adopt and immerse themselves into a foreign culture.
Geocentric: Individuals keep their own cultural attributes, but adjust to the culture of the country they live in.

When doing business in any other culture, there are many cross-cultural challenges that need to be addressed. For example, due to the extreme population boom, industry growth, and technological advantages, China has become a market in which many foreign companies are investing. Many Westerners experience tremendous difficulty when trying to conduct business in China because the two cultures are quite different. The cultural barriers such as difficulty of communication, different objectives and means of cooperation, and operating methods by each side, have led to failed business collaborations. The differences between China and the United States are not only due to cultural aspects, but also to differences in economic systems, political systems, social values, and laws.

As cross-cultural misunderstandings become more prevalent throughout the world, it becomes more important for international businesses to be aware of cultural differences. It is also important for international managers to learn how to deal with cultural misunderstandings and cross-cultural differences around the world. It is imperative for hiring managers for overseas operations to consider those individuals with geocentric tendencies and avoid ethnocentric individuals. It should be emphasized that cultural convergence among citizens of the world is occurring, especially among the highly skilled and educated classes. Through cultural convergence there is a certain degree of similarity in lifestyles, ways of living together, and even in value systems. Additionally, many people around the world are learning English. For example, in China it is required that high school graduates have English language knowledge.

If the citizens of a country such as the United States could be divided into two broad groups—highly educated and highly skilled to less educated and low skilled—cultural convergence would be observable in the highly educated and highly skilled group in different countries. In other words, a new phenomenon is observable: global cultural convergence and national/local divergence. This type of segmentation has many economic, political, and cultural implications. For example, the presidential elections in several developed countries and the United States are typically decided by 2% to

3% of the votes. Generally, landslide elections have become less frequent in many developed countries. One important factor of such electoral results is the phenomenon of national convergence/divergence.

3

The International Trade System

In this chapter, the general structure of the international trading system is described. The concept of free trade and its implications are discussed as well. The main theories of international trade are presented, as they are what provide scientific arguments for the free trade system. Finally, the concept of dynamic shifts in competitive advantage is introduced.

The Global Trade System

Trade between countries is one of the oldest business activities. International trade theorists have developed several frameworks for policy analysis and evaluation of the impact of trade on the participants. International trade also impacts a country's economic growth, employment, and inflations rates.

In general, importing countries obtain products at lower costs than the equivalent ones produced domestically, and exporting countries tend to benefit from the job creation and revenues generated from the growth of their exporting industries. In addition, multinational enterprises (MNEs) usually benefit from the profit margin generated by export-import activities.

Foundations of Global Business, pages 35–50
Copyright © 2016 by Information Age Publishing
All rights of reproduction in any form reserved.

Therefore, trade seems to benefit the countries as well as the multinational companies involved.

Table 3.1 shows the world's exports and the change in the export share in billions of USD from each region in the past 20 years. It can be seen that world trade has expanded considerably, particularly in the last two decades.

Between 1983 and 2013 world trades have been significant, which is due to the globalization of economies. A great deal of the increase in trade can be attributed to the increase of exports from Asian countries. This increase has been at the expense of North America and Western Europe. The share of Asian exports in the world increased from approximately 24% in 1983 to 38% in 2013, while the share of U.S. and European exports both declined in this period.

International trade has evolved to be truly a global trading system in which many countries all over the globe participate. For example, after the former Soviet Union collapsed at the end of the 1980s, many satellite countries in Eastern Europe and Central Asia suddenly became part of the international trading system. Countries such as the Czech Republic, Poland, Slovakia, Romania, and Hungary, among many others, have successfully joined the global trading system since then. The benefit has been higher economic growth and an improvement in the standard of living in these countries.

Many other countries such as Guatemala, Honduras, El Salvador, Nicaragua, and Costa Rica that initially adhered to the theory of import

TABLE 3.1   World and Regional Exports in Billion USD

	1983	1993	2003	2013
World	2,168	4,742	9,352	23,189
Developing economies	574	1,246	2,919	9,814
Transition economies	59	108	247	970
Developed economies	1,536	3,388	6,186	12,405
Developing economies: Africa	96	122	230	688
Developing economies: America	126	208	458	1,303
Developing economies: Asia	349	911	2,224	7,810
Developed economies: America	350	812	1,355	2,822
Developed economies: Asia	176	427	569	928
Developed economies: Europe	979	2,081	4,143	8,298
EU27 (European Union)	910	1,948	3,907	7,772
NAFTA (North American Free Trade Agreement)	380	874	1,532	3,220

Note: Exports and imports of goods and services in billion USD (Source: http://unctadstat. unctad.org/TableViewer/tableView.aspx?ReportId=25116)

substitution as the foundation of their economic development policy also changed this approach and joined the global trade system. Other countries such as China, India, and Brazil that had focused on self-sufficiency and internally focused on economic development until the 1990s have also become part of the global trading system. The economic growth and economic development of these particular countries has risen dramatically since the incorporation into the global trading system, and nowadays they hold the status of emerging countries or emerging market economies.

The global trading system incorporates the following aspects called pillars as shown in Figure 3.1:

1. The philosophy of free trade
2. The institutions that aid in the implementation of free trade
3. The concept of fair trade
4. Regional economic integration

Free Trade

The first pillar of the current global trading system is the belief that an open and free trade system is better than a system of managed trade with government involvement. This argument is based on a number of different principles (Meier, 1968). Free trade will lead to a shift in the resources of a nation to the products that can be produced relatively more efficiently as compared to other countries and thus export those products. In turn, products that cannot be produced efficiently relative to their trading

Figure 3.1 Pillars of the global trade system.

partners will be imported. This is the basis for the theory of comparative advantage (Appleyard, Field, & Cobb, 2010). The basic assumption of this theory is that individuals are best positioned to make decisions about the choices for product consumption. Therefore any government intervention in international trade through tariff and nontariff barriers affects the price structure and influences consumer choices. That is bureaucratic decision makers who may or may not represent the optimal choice of citizens influence the system.

Free trade will lead to an increase in the output of the system and an increase in global production and consumption. Since the standard of living improves with an increase in consumption, free trade leads to an improvement in the global standard of living.

Even though the goal of most countries is free trade, structurally there are issues such as the special interests of various groups within each country that can potentially make trade negotiations difficult. Considering the number of countries in the world and their own particular interests, it would be virtually impossible to negotiate an acceptable and comprehensive trade regime for all parties. Therefore, the observed trend has been the development of regional trading blocs. Negotiations among participants in the trading blocs have become the norm. For example, in the case of the European Union, the degree of integration has expanded beyond the usual economic trade and investment to include political integration.

Trade Theories

Theory of Absolute Advantage

Adam Smith developed the *theory of absolute advantage* in 1776. He argued that countries should specialize in the production of the goods they can produce at absolutely lower costs in terms of resources used. At the same time, countries should import products that would be more costly to produce. In addition, this theory states that by specializing in those industries, the productivity would increase, which in turn would lead to higher amounts of trade and a better economic situation for the countries involved.

Adam Smith also described two advantages a country could have: natural and acquired advantage. The natural advantage is determined by factors such as the climatic conditions, the access to certain natural resources, or the availability of an abundant labor force. Acquired advantages refer to those advantages developed in either production or process technology.

Theory of Comparative Advantage

David Ricardo developed the *theory of comparative advantage* in 1817 as an extension of the *theory of absolute advantage*. Ricardo's theory explains why there are benefits from trade between two countries, even when one of the countries has *absolute advantage* in the production of all goods (i.e., that country produces all products more efficiently than the other). The key assumptions of the theory of comparative advantage are:

1. Absence of government intervention
2. Perfect competition
3. Prices reflect the cost of production
4. Difference in factor endowment
5. Difference in the intensity of use of production factors in the production of each good
6. Mobility of factors of production
7. Full employment

The theory of comparative advantage is built on the concept of opportunity cost. This means that each country has a certain amount of productive resources such as labor, capital, and natural resources that should be used in the production of goods that can be produced most efficiently relative to its trading partners. Production of any other goods would use resources that could have been used more efficiently and therefore there is an opportunity cost in using those resources.

The issue of efficiency can be further articulated by the concept of economies of scale.[1] There are countries that are relatively small in size and therefore cannot achieve economies of scale in their production without international trade and export. These countries, by specialization, can reach economies of scale and reduce the cost of production. For example South Korea and Sweden are too small in terms of population to support a large auto industry. Each country has two car manufacturing companies that rely mainly on car exports.

Factor Proportion Theory

The question of what determines the comparative advantage of a country was further explored by Eli Heckscher and Bertil Ohlin in the Heckscher–Ohlin (H–O) theory of international trade. The *factor proportion theory* proposed by H–O argues that various countries have different endowments of various factors of production. At the same time, various products use different factors of production with different intensity. Therefore, based on this theory, a country would be exporting products that use intensively the abundant factor of production they have. In turn, a country would import products that use factors of production not available or less abundant within the country. For example, India would export labor-intensive products because of its large labor pool, while Western European countries would export products that are capital intensive. For example, Germany produces and exports automobiles and other highly technical products to the rest of the world.

Countries with abundant labor resources can export labor-intensive products. However, their situation in the long run is different from the countries with abundant capital resource. Countries with the labor cost advantage can export labor-intensive products that create more demand for labor. Since the population of a country is limited, a high demand for labor will drive up the costs of labor and make it less competitive for labor-intensive products. Therefore, the labor cost advantage is only a short-term advantage. However, countries with capital advantage can enjoy a long-term growth because they will have low cost of capital and will be competitive in capital-intensive products. Therefore, these countries can export capital-intensive products. Unlike labor-intensive products, exports of capital-intensive products will increase the capital supply due to the inflow of capital from export. Therefore, countries with capital advantages will have more capital supply from exporting capital-intensive products.

One of the implications of the factor proportion theory is the *law of one price*. The law of one price argues that as international trade takes place, the price of all goods will become the same across various borders. The only difference between the prices of goods among various locations would be due to the cost of transportation and insurance. If there is a price differential for goods between various locations, then there would be a flow of the good from the low price location to the higher price location until equilibrium is reached. This theory assumes the absence of government intervention in the market and that the exchange rate is at equilibrium based on purchasing power parity (Heller, 1968).

The law of one price further argues that the adjustment process will lead to the tendency for equalization of not only the price of goods, but also the price of factors of production. Labor endowed countries export products that use labor intensively. This will lead to an increase in the demand for labor and in turn, higher wages in those countries. Countries with abundant labor will export labor-intensive products and import capital-intensive products. On the other hand, countries that have a shortage of labor relative to capital (capital abundant countries) and high wages, will import labor-intensive products. This results in less demand for labor and a more moderate raise in wages, or even a decline in wages. This process leads toward the equalization of wages and at the same time it leads toward the equalization of the cost of capital (Samuelson, 1939, 1948)1939, 1948.

Yet comparative advantage is not static, but rather it changes over time. Many countries have attempted to change their comparative advantage from labor to technology and knowledge intensive industry. The technology and knowledge intensive industries by nature have higher value added, which is defined as the incremental input in terms of labor, capital, and resources and leads to higher per capita incomes. For example, in the 1960s Japan was viewed as a country with cheap labor, but by the mid 1980s its comparative advantage had shifted to the technology intensive industry sector and their per capita income was at the same level as the per capita income of the United States and Western European countries. Japan had the second highest GDP after the United States by late 1990s (Vernon, 1966). Another example is South Korea that also managed to transform its economy from a labor abundant to a technology rich one and began exporting advanced manufacturing products such as computers, telecommunication equipment, and automobiles. These countries developed their competitive advantage by building their research and development capabilities, improving management, and by developing knowledge intensive industries (Bhagwati, Panagariya, & Srinivasan, 1998; Daniels, Radebaugh, & Sullivan, 2012).

Benefits of Trade

A simple example demonstrates the gains from international trade. To keep the example simple, a set of assumptions is made. While none of the simplifying assumptions are critical in the demonstration of gain from trade, without the assumptions a more complex mathematical or graphical model would be needed.

Assume that there are two countries, America (A) and Britain (B), and two different products, Wheat (W) and Cloth (C). Using all its factors of production, A can produce 50 units of W or 100 units of C. On the other hand, B using all its resources can produce 20 units of W and 60 units of C.

	America (A)	Britain (B)
Wheat (W)	50	20
Cloth (C)	100	60

The price ratios for each country are the following:

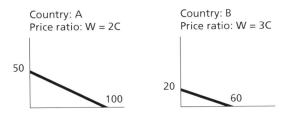

Country: A
Price ratio: W = 2C

Country: B
Price ratio: W = 3C

Effectively, for country A, for every unit of Wheat produced, they can get 2 units of Cloth. That means that by producing 1 unit of Wheat, they are giving up the production of 2 units of Cloth. For country B, the price ratio is higher, since for every unit of Wheat produced, they could get 3 units of Cloth. Again, they are giving up the production of 3 units of Cloth in order to produce 1 unit of Wheat.

From this analysis it is obvious A is comparatively more efficient than B in the production of Wheat. Consequently, Country A will specialize in producing Wheat, while Country B will specialize on Cloth.

Let's see what the result of trade between these two countries would be (Table 3.2).

TABLE 3.2   Results of Trade Between Countries A and B

	A		B	
	Wheat	**Cloth**	**Wheat**	**Cloth**
Autarky				
Production	25	50	10	30
Consumption	25	50	10	30
With Trade at A term of trade: C = 2W				
Production	50	0	0	60
Consumption	25			30
Export	25			30
Import		50	15	
Gain	0	0	5	0
With Trade at B term of trade: C = 3W				
Production	50	0	0	60
Consumption	25			30
Export	25			30
Import		75	10	
Gain	0	25	0	0

A and B allocate resources in autarky (no trade) to produce half W and half C and would consume that amount A (25, 50) & B (10, 30). After trade, A produces 50 W according to its comparative advantage and B 60 C. They consume the same amount of what they produced in autarky and trade the remaining.

With A's term of trade, A exports 25 units of W and can import 50 C. B exports 30 units of C and brings 15 units of W. Country A is not worse off, but country B is better off since it consumes 5 more units of Wheat. There is a net global gain as a result of trade.

With B's term of trade, A exports 25 units of W and imports 75 units of C. B exports 30 units of C and imports 10 units of W. Country A is better off since it consumes 25 more units of C while country B is not worse off. Once again, we observe a net gain due to trade.

Specialization along the lines of comparative advantage increases global welfare as demonstrated by the increase in consumption. Each country would like to have terms of trade equal to those of their trading partner's domestic prices. In reality, prices would be between the two country's domestic price ratios and both countries would gain. A price ratio outside this limit would result in losses for one of the countries as a result of trade. In that case, a country would refuse to trade.

Reasons for Government Intervention

The trade theories discussed previously assume that there is no government intervention. However, in reality there is always some level of government intervention in trade. Government intervention, however, will result in the distortion of the price structure. Governments use several arguments to justify their intervention in international trade. The main arguments for intervention are the following:

1. Protecting domestic employment: High unemployment is very undesirable for any government. The import of cheaper products from low-wage countries may result in the closure of some local noncompetitive firms. This, in turn, may lead to an increase in unemployment.
2. Protecting domestic industry: Similarly, governments try to protect local industries against foreign competitors who might be able to produce the same goods more competitively and at cheaper prices because of lower labor costs. However, these arguments fail to recognize that there are gains from specialization based on

their comparative advantages. Protectionism many times results in inefficient industries and low per capita income reflecting low marginal productivity in low value added industries. Shifting resources to the industries in which a country has a comparative advantage and where labor productivity is high will improve the wage structure as well as the standard of living in the long run.

For example, textile firms in China can produce and sell low-end products at lower costs than the United States. If the United States had protected the textile industry in the last century, then the value of the workers and their wages in that industry would have been the same as that of China. By permitting the textile industry to move overseas, the resources, including labor, were shifted to other industries. In New England, for example, a number of new industries eventually replaced the textile industry. Industries such as electronic, bio-tech, and software created much higher paying jobs and improved the standard of living in the region. Obviously, it took a number of years for such a transformation to happen.

3. Controlling the balance of payments: This type of trade intervention is typical of countries with balance of payments difficulties that seek to reduce imports in order to decrease the trade deficit. Trying to reduce imports by implementing trade barriers is not the best solution to eliminate a trade deficit since it implies that the government is making decisions on behalf of society and distorting the price structure. The alternative, and a much better policy from the market perspective, is to eliminate tariffs and devaluate the exchange rate so that the government does not introduce bias into the consumption pattern of society.

4. Supplementing government income: Imposing import taxes and tariffs represents an easy and effective way of collecting funds for the government. Following the same reasoning as above, intervening in trade by applying import taxes and tariffs means creating a bias in the consumption pattern and artificially manipulating the consumers' choices. A preferred policy would be for the government to organize an equitable and effective tax system and collection process.

5. Protecting infant industry: This intervention considers applying taxes to foreign products in order to help the local industry to develop and attain economies of scale. This intervention is mostly implemented in developing countries, in order to help an *infant* industry grow and develop until it can compete in a global market. This argument makes sense and seems like a good solution to help infant industries, particularly in emerging markets. However,

the drawback is that in the long run, those industries get accustomed to being protected and cannot compete in an open market when the protection disappears. Effectively, infant industry protection leads to inefficient industries once they are not protected.

6. Political objectives: In this case we find countries applying restrictions for political reasons. One example is the trade sanctions imposed on Cuba by the United States. The economic and trade sanctions that were imposed on Cuba after Castro took power in 1962 aimed to undermine the regime. Unfortunately, the trade sanctions have not succeeded in bringing a regime change in Cuba. The free trade theory argues that if the above-mentioned policies are the second best solutions for achieving their objective, then we must look for the best policies since the second best is an inferior approach. The exceptions are infant industry protection and national security concerns. According to second best theory, the second best policy is an inferior policy; if the best policy is not adopted, there is no second best. (Bennear & Stavins, 2007; Lipsey & Lancaster, 1956)

Tariff and Nontariff Barriers' Impacts

There are two ways governments can interfere in international trade: through tariff and nontariff barriers. A tariff is a tax applied either on exported or imported goods. The import tariff is considered to be the easiest way to collect the tax, since a product cannot enter the country unless this tax is paid. The two main types of tariffs are:

Specific tariff: It is a fixed fee per unit of import. Effectively, it is a fee paid for every good imported and it is unchanging and unique, which means it does not change depending on the value of the good. Therefore, these tariffs have to be revised once in a while to adjust them to inflation or changes in the economic situation of the country.

Example: The payment of $5 per barrel of oil imported. In the 1988 presidential election there was a proposal by one of the candidates to reduce U.S. dependence on imported oil by imposing a $5 fee on imported oil.

Ad valorem tariff: It is a percentage of the value of the import. This type of tariff is usually more problematic to implement since it can vary constantly depending on changes in the value of the imported good.

Example: The payment of 10% of the value of an imported car.

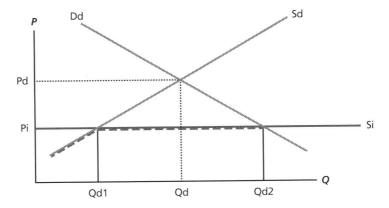

Figure 3.2 Market equilibrium without tariff.

The impact of a tariff is evident and affects the equilibrium of the supply and demand (Dd and Sd) in the market (see Figure 3.2). Let's analyze the situation in a market without a tariff. In a country with autarky, a condition of economic self-sufficiency, the equilibrium between domestic supply and domestic demand would be (Pd, Qd) respectively. Effectively, Pd would be the domestic price and Qd the domestic consumption. Let's assume the country imports products from abroad. In that case, Si will be the international supply. Qd1 is the amount of consumption of domestic products (domestic production). Qd2 – Qd1, therefore, represents the amount of consumption of international products or the imports.

Let's now take a look at the change in the equilibrium when applying a tariff on imports (see Figure 3.3). In that case, the international price rises

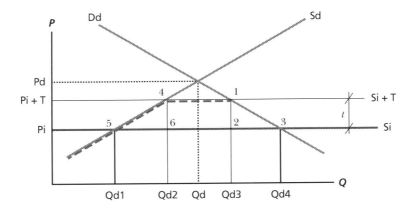

Figure 3.3 Market equilibrium with tariff.

proportionally with the tariff imposed (T). Therefore, domestic production increases to Qd2. Therefore, Qd3 – Qd2 is the amount of imports, which is considerably reduced compared to the amount of imports in the previous example. Effectively, Qd4 – Qd3 is the decline in the number of imports and also the decline in consumption due to the tariff, and Qd2 – Qd1 is the increase in domestic production due to the tariff.

The triangle (123) represents the loss of consumer surplus, while triangle (456) is the loss of producer surplus. In this scenario, the government income is calculated by (Q3 – Q2) × T.

Nontariff Barriers

There are other ways, besides tariffs, in which governments intervene in international trade. These are called nontariff barriers.

Import quota: This is the most common import restriction and consists of setting an upper limit on the amount of goods that can be imported for a certain period of time. This type of trade intervention affects the international supply in a direct way as compared with the effects of tariffs. Effectively, tariffs are applied, but consumers determine the amount of international consumption in the market. Contrarily, import quotas restrict and directly determine the amount of products that are going to be imported to the country. There are a number of other nontariff barriers such as ISO 9000 standards, bill of origin, cultural liability of foreignness, etc.

While tariffs and quotas may help specific segments of the economy, namely the producers within protected sectors of the economy in the short term, it is a benefit at the expense of the consumers. Consumers pay higher prices and most likely would consume fewer products due to the higher prices. Tariffs and quotas also reduce the overall welfare of the economy by reducing consumer surplus. The discussion of welfare economics is beyond the scope of this text.

The International Institution of Free Trade: WTO

The World Trade Organization (WTO) was the reincarnation of the General Agreement of Tariffs and Trade (GATT) that was established much earlier. The WTO was established in 1995 in Geneva, Switzerland. As of 2015, it has 161 members (WTO, 2014a). The major objective of the organization is to create common agreements that dictate what the trade regulations among its members are.

WTO has defined its mission as:

> The WTO provides a forum for negotiating agreements aimed at reducing obstacles to international trade and ensuring a level playing field for all, thus contributing to economic growth and development. The WTO also provides a legal and institutional framework for the implementation and monitoring of these agreements, as well as for settling disputes arising from their interpretation and application. (WTO, 2014b)

The first steps for the creation of the WTO were taken in Bretton Woods, New Hampshire, in 1944 with the establishment of the International Trade Organization (ITO). The organization did not succeed and only one of its agreements persisted, the GATT. After several negotiations that took place between 1986 and 1995, the WTO was created, undertaking part of the GATT principles.

The final aim of the WTO is to increase smooth, free, fair, and predictable trade among countries. The organization accomplishes that by:

- Administrating trade agreements
- Acting as a forum for trade negotiations
- Settling trade disputes
- Reviewing national trade policies
- Assisting developing countries in trade policy issues
- Cooperating with other international organizations

Nowadays, 97% of world trade is represented by the WTO through its 161 country members. Furthermore, around 30 countries are currently negotiating to join the organization. All the country members approve all the decisions.

The structure of the WTO is quite complex. There are four organizational levels with their respective bodies. The most important one is the Ministerial Conference, which meets once every 2 years and is responsible for major decisions affecting the countries in the organization. The General Council belongs to the second level of bodies and is responsible for the work of the Ministerial Conference on a daily basis. On the third level, there are three different councils: the Councils for Trade that focus on the three different trade areas (goods, intellectual property rights, and services). Finally, the three subsidiary bodies that report to each one of the councils form the fourth level.

Fair Trade

The main purpose of the so-called fair trade approach is to help producers in developing countries to have better working and trading conditions, and to promote sustainability. Fair trade can be considered a social movement that is market based. The movement advocates for the payment of higher prices to local producers as well as higher social and environmental standards from multinational enterprises. The fair trade movement focuses in particular on exports from developing countries to developed countries, such as handicrafts and agricultural products like coffee and cocoa.

In 2008, the Fairtrade Labelling Organizations International (FLO) estimated that more than 7.5 million producers and their families were benefiting from fair trade funded infrastructure, technical assistance, and community development projects. Products certified with FLO International's fair trade certification amounted to approximately $4.98 billion worldwide, a 22% year-to-year increase (FTI, 2014). While this represents a tiny fraction of world trade in physical merchandise, some fair trade products account for 20% to 50% of all sales in their product categories in individual countries (WTO, 2010).

The response to fair trade has been mixed. Fair trade's increasing popularity has drawn criticism from both ends of the political spectrum. The Adam Smith Institute sees fair trade as a type of subsidy or marketing ploy that impedes growth (Munger, 2014). Segments of the left, such as French author Christian Jacquiau, criticize fair trade for not adequately challenging the current trading system (Hamel, 2006).

Conclusion

The global trading system has changed over time due to the new institutional structure such as the emergence of the World Trade Organization, new rules of international trade, and new competitors in the world such as China and India that offer cheap labor. Yet, the underlying philosophy of free trade is still intact and more countries such as China, Vietnam, and others are joining the system and adopting it. The debate, however, has shifted to concerns about how the system can be made more fair and equitable. In other words, the discussion has been expanded from the concept of efficiency and comparative advantage presented by neo-classical economists to now include the concept of fairness as discussed in this chapter.

Note

1. Paul Krugman: http://www.nobelprize.org/nobel_prizes/economics/laureates/2008/

4

Economic Integration

This chapter discusses the forces that drive economic integration. In addition, the benefits and disadvantages of economic integration are identified. The major existing trade agreements are also discussed. Finally, the chapter analyzes the effects of economic integration on foreign direct investment (FDI).

Economic Integration through Regionalization

Far from taking place in a single global market, more than 80% of foreign direct investment (FDI) and over half of the world trade takes place in regional blocks (Rugman, 2012). As regional trade agreements and arrangements have increased over the past three decades, determining the precise cause of their proliferation and their effects on the economy and on policies has been a challenge for economists, international business scholars, and policymakers. Even though some integration agreements have been motivated by political considerations, more often the driving force for such agreements is economics. In the short term, integration is expected to

Foundations of Global Business, pages 51–64
Copyright © 2016 by Information Age Publishing

stimulate intraregional trade and investment; in the longer term, it is believed that the combination of larger markets, tougher competition, more efficient resource allocation, and various positive externalities will increase the growth rates of participating economies.

The relation between trade agreements and foreign direct investment (FDI) is multidimensional in nature making system dynamics a better approach to analyze the relationship rather than static studies. The FDI impact varies depending on the character of existing foreign direct investment in a certain country. The FDI investment can be categorized as horizontal, which refers to multinational enterprises (MNEs) manufacturing products and providing services that are similar to those the multinational produces in its home market and other foreign markets; and vertical investment, which refers to those multinationals that fragment production processes geographically.

Another known classification is the import-substituting investment, which emphasizes the replacement of some agricultural or industrial imports to encourage local production for domestic consumption in order to increase industrialization; and export-oriented investment that aims at industrialization through creating competitive advantage by specializing in certain products. Finally, integration between developed countries differs from integration between developing countries depending on how competitive and complementary the economies are (Blomstrom & Kokko, 1997).

Tariff reductions are usually important provisions of trade agreements. The inflows of FDI could go up if the average level of protection decreases as a result of the trade agreement. This surge of inward FDI would not necessarily be evenly distributed, but rather it would be concentrated in the geographical areas with the strongest locational advantages (Yeyati, Stein, & Daude, 2003). In addition, internalization theories imply that inflows of FDI are likely to increase as a result of regional integration since a larger market makes the region a more attractive investment location (Buckley & Casson, 1976; Dunning, 1976; Stiglitz, 2007).

Types of Trade Agreements

Economic integration has been an important dimension of international trade and investment. The different levels of economic integration (see Figure 4.1) between countries are the following:

■ **Bilateral trade agreement:** This type of trade agreement is either between two nations, between a nation and a trading bloc, or be-

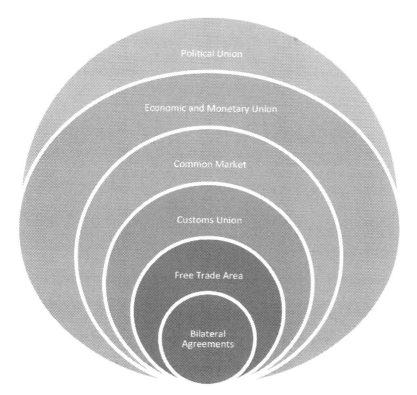

Figure 4.1 Levels of integration.

tween two trading blocs. The objective of a bilateral agreement is to give the parties involved a favored trading status between each other. The following are examples of bilateral trade agreements: the Mexico–Israel free trade agreement and the Japan–Singapore free trade agreement.

■ **Free trade area (FTA):** In this case, countries abolish all tariffs on goods among them, while maintaining an individual external tariff against non-FTA economies. Tariffs or quotas are eliminated on most or all of the products. Countries normally establish a time period to implement the changes. One of the most well-known examples of a free trade area is the North American Free Trade Agreement (NAFTA), comprised of Canada, Mexico, and the United States that came into effect in 1994. Other examples are the South Asia Free Trade Agreement (SAFTA), the Common Market for Eastern and Southern Africa (COMESA), and the ASEAN Free Trade Area (AFTA), which is the free trade zone among the Association of Southeast Asian Nations (ASEAN). A very common practice in FTAs is the establishment of "rules of origin," which consists of identifying where the product comes from with the objective of avoiding duty evasion through re-exportation of products.

▪ **Customs union:** The major difference between a FTA and a customs union is the fact that in addition to eliminating internal tariffs among members, countries also have common tariffs against nonmembers. Unlike the FTA, where every country keeps their own external tariffs, in this case countries agree on a common external trade policy. A well-known customs union is the Mercado Común del Sur (or Mercosur in Spanish), which means Southern Common Market. Mercosur consists of Argentina, Brazil, Paraguay, Uruguay, and Venezuela.

▪ **Common market:** In this case, in addition to the characteristics of a customs union, there is also free mobility of factors of production (land, labor and capital) among the members of the common market. The objective is that the movement of those factors is free inside of the area. The European Union, which officially became a single market in 1996 with the signature of the Maastricht Treaty, is the most well-known and established common market.

▪ **Economic and monetary union:** The EMU is a common market with a shared currency. The largest EMU right now is the Eurozone, which consists of a group of European Union members who have adopted the euro as the official currency. In addition to that, members also share the same economic policy, meaning that key macroeconomic decisions are no longer taken by each individual country, but are centralized. In the case of the European Union, the European Central Bank (ECB) is responsible for the monetary policy in the area.

▪ **Political union:** This is the maximum level of integration among countries and occurs when a group of states adopts not only common economic and monetary practices, but also a common political policy. One of the examples is the United Arab Emirates (UAE).

Winners and Losers from Economic Integration

There are sociocultural, political, and economic changes associated with economic integration. The static effects and, to a lesser extent, the dynamic effects caused by increasing levels of integration among economies are the most common effects studied.

Static effects refer to the shift in the allocation of resources from less efficient economies to more efficient ones. Dynamic effects refer to the overall growth experienced by an economy due to the accessibility to a new, larger market share and factors of input.

It is believed that static effects take place when one of the following two situations occurs:

- Trade creation: This is the overall positive effect on trade caused by higher levels of economic integration. It occurs when there is an increase in the amount of trade as a result of shifts in resource allocation. In this case, production moves to more efficient participants in the common trade area, replacing other less efficient producers, for reasons of comparative advantage. Free trade implies no protection for national producers. Therefore, companies that before joining a trade agreement were facing difficulties with exporting to other "protected" countries can now do so without any problem or tariffs. Increased efficiency in production leads to higher demand and, consequently, to more trade and economic growth. The downside part of trade creation is for those companies whose demand declines as a consequence of comparative advantage. In a nonprotected environment they will have to learn how to compete with more efficient producers, who might be using factors of production less costly or in a more efficient way.
- Trade diversion: This might be considered the main drawback of economic integration, although it also leads to economic growth for the member countries. Trade diversion occurs when trade shifts from nonmember participants to member countries as a result of the elimination of trade barriers. In this case, the shift might be occurring not because the member countries are more efficient than the nonmembers, but because the nonexistence of trade barriers makes it cheaper to import within the free trade zone. The immediate loser in trade diversion is, obviously, the nonmember country, since it is losing market share at the expense of member participants. However, in reality there is an overall loss for all participants, since trade diversion means that less efficient products are being traded, contrary to what the theory of comparative advantage states.

For example, when NAFTA was created there were concerns that trade diversion would happen as a consequence of the trade agreement, shifting exports and imports from nonmember countries to NAFTA members. However, later studies have demonstrated that there has not been a significant trade diversion (Fukao, Okubo, & Stern, 2003). For instance, Mexico's exports from 1991 to 2001 to non-NAFTA markets increased as much as its exports to the United States and Canada.

NAFTA

The North America Free Trade Agreement (NAFTA) went into effect on January 1, 1994. The trade agreement allows the free trade of products, services, and investments between Canada, the United States, and Mexico. Prior to this, the amount of trade taking place between the United States and Canada was already the largest amount of trade between two countries in the world. Before NAFTA was signed, the United States was the largest importer of products from both Canada (85.8%) and Mexico (88.9%). These two countries imported about 30% of the exports from the United States. It made sense to remove the barriers to trade to allow the trade to expand. In 1993, there were $4 billion in foreign investments that flowed into Mexico. By 1999, the flow of FDI to Mexico reached $11.8 billion.

This was a very controversial agreement with a lot of resistance from the unions and environmentalists in the United States. The unions were afraid that U.S. companies would relocate manufacturing to Mexico due to the low wages and lax environmental laws, resulting in huge job losses in the United States. The unions joined forces with the environmentalists, who were concerned about the lack of laws and lax enforcement of the existing laws regarding environmental protection. As a result of the tremendous pressure to address these concerns, three provisions were added to the agreement dealing with workers' rights, environmental protection, and a means for dispute resolution. NAFTA includes more provisions than standard free trade agreements because of the additional clauses.

In addition, a rule of origin provision with specific limits was established. In most cases, 50% of the net value of a product must originate in North America. Exceptions are footwear (55%), automobiles, light-weight trucks, the engines and transmissions for these vehicles (62.5%), and 60% for other vehicles and auto parts. Commercial or customs invoices must accompany the products to prove the items meet these guidelines.

Some of the predicted outcomes of this agreement have come true and some have not. As predicted, manufacturing companies have rationalized their products, production, and investments in the NAFTA region. This is especially true in the automotive industry. Employment in the automotive industry increased in the United States after NAFTA. The production is dispersed throughout the region covered by NAFTA. Some other industries such as the furniture and apparel industries relocated their production to Mexico.

It was also predicted that many Mexican and Canadian companies would not be able to compete with the more sophisticated American companies and would be forced out of business. This prediction did not turn out to be correct. Many of the companies were able to reorganize and re-strategize in a way that made them more efficient and more competitive. However, this has not been true in every case. For example, the Mexican retailers have not been able to compete with huge retailers, such as Walmart and Carrefour.

Due to increased competition from America, 1.3 million agricultural jobs were lost in Mexico. Many of those workers crossed the border illegally into the United States and took low-wage jobs to regularly send money back to their families in Mexico. As a result of NAFTA, more U.S. companies moved their operations to Mexico. Many companies that were operating in Asia relocated facilities to Mexico to take advantage of the relatively low cost of labor and the easy access and lower transportation costs needed to sell to the U.S. market. As wages in Mexico rise, more companies are moving production out of Mexico to lower-wage areas, such as Vietnam and Cambodia. This effect has been compounded by the recent drop in textile quotas by the WTO. As wages continue to rise and people have more discretionary spending, foreign countries will begin to view Mexico as a consumer market instead of a production location.

CAFTA-DR

The Central American Free Trade Agreement, most commonly known as CAFTA-DR, is a free trade agreement between the United States and five Central American countries (Guatemala, El Salvador, Honduras, Nicaragua, and Costa Rica) and the Dominican Republic. The treaty was signed in 2004 (USTR, 2005).

CAFTA is considered to be the first subregional agreement to be signed between such disparate economies. The combined gross domestic product (GDP) of the five Central American countries and the Dominican Republic is approximately a half percent (0.5%) of the GDP of the United States. CAFTA-DR provisions require that the majority of goods and services are deregulated. Some of these goods and services in Central America include agricultural products, manufactured products, public services such as health care, energy (electricity), and other sectors that were traditionally state monopolies such as telecommunications and the financial sector. In return, the United States has pledged to increase the market access for textiles and agricultural products like sugar (Hornbeck, 2005a).

In addition, this free trade agreement also provides the United States a chance to pursue other issues of commercial importance such as intellectual property rights, foreign investment, environmental and labor regulations, government procurement, e-commerce, and financial services (Hornbeck, 2005b).

From the Central American perspective, the reduction of barriers in trade to their largest export market (which is the United States) and the ability to increase the attraction of foreign direct investment were significant incentives to proceed with the treaty. It is expected that CAFTA-DR will potentially increase not only U.S. foreign direct investment in the region, but also from the rest of the world.

Debate

Supporters of CAFTA-DR stressed that strategic and geopolitical issues must be considered. The treaty has the potential of reinforcing stability through the provisions that mandate the creation and development of legal frameworks and institutional structures that support democracy. If such structures and frameworks are in place, the rule of law would prevail and narco-trafficking and organized crime would be deterred.

On the other hand, doubters of CAFTA-DR have expressed their concerns about issues related to the increasing economic inequality that is reflected in the widening gap between the rich and poor. Globalization and economic integration are considered the culprits of the observed disparity in the society. Therefore, a free trade agreement would maintain the structures that cause the economic inequality and could even worsen the status quo. For this reason, it is common to find in recently negotiated treaties the inclusion of provisions for equitable labor conditions and provisions to prevent environmental degradation by increasing environmental protection.

The CAFTA-DR trade agreement includes a comprehensive legal framework of provisions to be implemented by the member countries. Using a system dynamics approach, the effects of tariff reductions and stronger protections for investors on FDI and on the workforce in industrial and agricultural sectors can be analyzed. Most of the current approaches and research are concerned with the static effects of regional integration agreements and policies on FDI flows. However, a system dynamics approach can be used to understand the effects and interactions of several CAFTA-DR provisions on FDI in all the different CAFTA-DR country members.

While implementation of CAFTA-DR was not uniform, all signatory countries have started implementing the agreement. Despite the treaty's implementation being under way, the debate on the agreement's merit continues. Supporters of CAFTA envision its implementation as the next step after the establishment of the North American Free Trade Agreement (NAFTA) toward achieving a hemispheric free trade agreement. On the other hand, opponents are not persuaded that the agreement will benefit all signatory countries and argue that it has not been established whether Central American signatories are economically and politically well suited for inclusion in this new free trade zone. Critics have questioned the advisability of adopting another free trade agreement in light of the United States' experience with NAFTA. Concerns range from potential negative effects on the economic competitiveness of Central American farmers to threats of further job losses faced by American manufacturing workers. Given these publicly expressed concerns, there has not been uniform support for CAFTA-DR's implementation. Furthermore, there are equally significant concerns about CAFTA-DR's nature and structure regarding its legal effects (Byrnes, 2007).

The CAFTA-DR agreement extended immediate duty free access to more than half of all U.S. agricultural exports. Average tariffs applied by the member countries to imports of agricultural products from the United States exceed 11% and on certain import sensitive products, can be more than 150%. Tariffs on the most sensitive agricultural products will be phased out over periods ranging from 5 to 20 years. Liberalization will be undertaken using tariff-rate quotas (Clark, 2009).

Some of the concerns about the negative impacts of the agreement are summarized in Table 4.1. The Economic Commission for Latin America and the Caribbean (ECLAC), as well as other institutions such as the Institute of Social Studies, have published several studies and reports on the impact of CAFTA on several member countries as well as the impact on different industrial sectors (Monge-González & González-Alvarado, 2007; Paunovic, 2005). The analysis tool used in these reports is the computable general equilibrium (CGE) modeling. Generally, the results of these reports are mixed and do not present polarizing statements.

TABLE 4.1 Potential Negative Impacts of CAFTA-DR

CAFTA Impacts in U.S.	CAFTA Impacts in Central America
Trade deficits rise and shifts in production overseas accelerate	Imports of staple crops and falling prices displace subsistence farmers
More U.S. jobs lost, particularly in manufacturing	New opportunities in export-oriented industries insufficient to absorb farmers and other workers displaced by imports
Downward pressure on wages intensifies and income inequality rises	Weakened rules on workers' rights prevent workers from organizing and pull down wages even in export sectors

The European Union

The need for the European Union (EU) stemmed from the devastation created during World War II. Political leaders realized they could accomplish a lot more and more quickly by working together to improve their economies. The cooperation has increased over the years, and the member countries are more and more intertwined with each other. This brings advantages as well as some challenges.

The Treaty of Maastricht

The Maastricht Treaty, signed in 1992, called for the establishment of a European economic, monetary, and political union. The political union involves a common European citizenship. It also involves joint foreign, defense, immigration, and policing policies. Harmonization of social policy on workers' issues was another goal of the treaty. Some countries such as France and Germany want closer European integration. Others, such as the United Kingdom and Denmark want less centralized control.

The European Monetary Union (EMU) is an umbrella term for the group of policies aimed at converging the economies of members of the European Union to adopt the euro (single currency). The term Eurozone is used interchangeably. The European Monetary System (EMS) is the system set up to create exchange rate stability in Europe, and the European Currency Unit (ECU) is a composite or basket of currencies in the EMS where each country's value is weighted according to economic strength and other factors.

Convergence Criteria

There are minimum criteria that a country must achieve prior to admittance to the EMU. The requirements are:

- Inflation must be held to within 1.5% of the rate of the top three countries.
- Long-term interest rates need to be controlled to within 2% of the interest rate of the top three countries with the lowest interest rates.
- The currency must be stabilized. For at least 2 years, the country needs to keep the currency fluctuations within the normal fluctuation margins of the European Exchange Rate Mechanism.
- The budget deficit, as a percent of Gross Domestic Product (GDP), must be less than or equal to 3% GDP. GDP is the value of production that occurs within a country's borders whether done by domestic or foreign factors of production.
- The public debt as a percent of GDP must be less than or equal to 60% GDP.

Key EU Institutions

European Monetary Institute (EMI)

This is the predecessor to the European Central Bank (ECB). It was established on January 1, 1994, to assist with the transition needed to meet the requirements of the Maastricht Treaty. It helped create the framework for a smooth transition to a single currency. Another function of the EMI was to assist with the legal framework needed so that people would have faith in existing contracts and that legal documents would remain valid under the new system. In its later stages, the EMI provided the infrastructure for business to continue between the member countries. Furthermore, it provided common standards (such as operating times, settlement times, etc.) for transactions to continue as the members moved toward the common currency. The EMI was dissolved when the ECB was formed.

European System of Central Banks (ESCB)

The ESCB consists of the European Central Bank (ECB) and the National Central Banks (NCB) of the 25 member countries. The ESCB functions to set monetary policy, perform foreign exchange transactions, offer a payment transaction system, and hold the foreign reserves of the member countries.

European Central Bank (ECB)

The ECB was formed on July 1, 1998, with the purpose of setting monetary policy and managing the exchange rate system. Other functions, added in 1999, are to coordinate the central bank activities of its member countries and to set monetary policy.

Major Problems

A major problem is the instability in currency values. As mentioned previously, in order to join the EMU, countries must minimize the fluctuations in their currency as compared to the euro. This has been a challenge for many potential members.

Another major obstacle is the inability to meet the required criteria, especially debt related criteria. Germany, France, and Italy have violated the budget deficit requirements for the past several years. As a result of this, the EU has not enforced the fines that were originally called for under these circumstances. There have been calls for reform of the requirements.

Governments struggle to make the needed social cuts that are required to meet the economic criteria for membership. These potential budget cuts for social services such as pensions, health care, and education are highly unpopular and implementing them can prove extraordinarily difficult.

Agricultural subsidiaries are another issue. This issue became more pressing as 10 new members joined in 2004. They have more employment dependent on agriculture than the other member countries. It will be expensive to get the farms of these countries up to the standards required by the Common Agricultural Policy (CAP).

The vastly different economies of EU members have different threats to their economies. For example, France and Germany, with slow growth and high unemployment rates, need low interest rates to hold down inflation and stimulate the economy. The United Kingdom and Denmark, on the other hand, have faster growth rates and low unemployment. They need higher interest rates to slow down the economy. Many of the new members have very high levels of unemployment. This conflicts with the actions of the European Central Bank whose objective is to keep inflation under control. This creates problems for some of the member countries that do not have control over their fiscal or monetary policy.

The 2010 European Sovereign Debt Crisis

The European sovereign crisis illustrates the financial, economic, and political interconnectedness of Europe. In early 2010, fears of a sovereign debt crisis concerning Greece, Ireland, Italy, Portugal, and Spain developed. Concerns about rising government deficits and debt levels across the globe, together with a wave of downgrading of European government debt, created alarm in financial markets. The debt crisis had been mostly centered on Greece, but it had repercussions throughout the region and beyond.

In May of 2010, the Eurozone countries and the International Monetary Fund agreed to a €110 billion loan for Greece, conditional on the implementation of harsh Greek austerity measures. Europe's finance ministers approved a comprehensive rescue package worth almost a trillion dollars aimed at ensuring financial stability across Europe by creating the European Financial Stability Facility (BBC News, 2010).

Causes of the Greek Government Funding Crisis

The Greek economy was one of the fastest growing in the Eurozone during the 2000s. A strong economy and falling bond yields allowed the government of Greece to run large structural deficits. After the introduction of the euro, Greece was initially able to borrow due to the lower interest rates government bonds could command. The global financial crisis that began in 2008 had a particularly large effect on Greece because two of the country's largest industries, tourism and shipping, were badly affected by the downturn with revenues falling 15% in 2009.

Without a bailout agreement, there was a possibility that Greece would have been forced to default on some of its debt. A default would most likely have taken the form of restructuring where Greece would pay creditors only a portion of what they were owed, perhaps 50% or 25%. This would have effectively removed Greece from the euro, as it would no longer have collateral with the European Central Bank. It would also destabilize the Euro Interbank Offered Rate, which is backed by government securities. However, the overall effect of a probable Greek default would itself have been small for the other European economies. Greece represents only 2.5% of the Eurozone economy. The more severe danger was that a default by Greece would cause investors to lose faith in other Eurozone countries. This concern was also focused on Portugal and Ireland, all of which have high debt and deficit issues. Italy also has a high debt, but its budget position is better than the European average, and it is not considered amongst the countries most at risk.

Figure 4.2 ▓ Greece, Italy, Portugal and Spain with ▓ Ireland with ▓ United Kingdom.

The crisis was seen as a justification for imposing fiscal austerity on Greece in exchange for European funding, which would lower borrowing costs for the Greek government. The negative impact of tighter fiscal policy could offset the positive impact of lower borrowing costs, and social disruption could have a significantly negative impact on investment and growth in the longer term.

Many questions can be asked and debated about this case. Here are a few questions:

What are the effects of the Greek crisis on the value of the euro? What are the effects of the crisis on Spain, Portugal and Italy? What is their effect on the rest of the Eurozone? What are the challenges that the EU is facing? What are the potential solutions? What is its implication for the rest of the world? What are the impacts of globalization on regionalization?

5

The Global Financial System

This chapter discusses the structure of the global financial system. The major institutions and workings of the international financial market are described. In addition, the functioning of the currency markets as well as the factors that impact exchange rates are discussed. Finally, the challenges that the global financial system faces are analyzed.

As shown in Figure 5.1, the global financial system (GFS) is defined by two components: global financial institutions and global financial markets. Global financial institutions include the International Monetary Fund (IMF), regional financial institutions, the World Bank, and regional development banks. The main function of these institutions is to help in the economic development of their members and to stabilize the financial and economic environment.

The global financial market consists of foreign exchange markets, international equity markets, and international debt markets. These markets extend beyond geographic boundaries for investment by bringing lenders and investors together irrespective of the geographic location.

Foundations of Global Business, pages 65–85
Copyright © 2016 by Information Age Publishing

Figure 5.1 Global financial system structure.

Global financial institutions such as the World Bank and the International Monetary Fund oversee the global economy from micro and macro perspectives and initiate and support policies that stabilize and grow the world economy. There are regional financial institutions such as the European Central Bank that focus on specific regions with the same aim. The main foci of the global financial markets are the foreign exchange market, the international equity market, the international debt market, and other financial instruments. The foreign exchange market deals with currency exchange transactions of various countries. Its mission is to bring together buyers and sellers of a currency.

The dynamic pattern of the GFS has been continuously improved in terms of the efficiency of global financial operations. This has been instrumental for consistent global economic growth. However, simultaneously, this has resulted in the transfer of risk across geographic boundaries. In other words, systemic risk of the financial market has become globalized.

Global Financial Institutions

Regarding the global financial institutions, some are truly international, such as the World Bank and the International Monetary Fund, which were set up initially after World War II as part of the Bretton Woods Agreement to manage and stabilize the global financial system. There are regional financial institutions such as the European Central Bank and the Asian Development Bank that focus on their respective regions. In addition, there are international banks that operate around the world and have their headquarters in specific countries. The main function of international banks is to provide value to their shareholders by providing a high rate of return and by diversifying risk. Finally, there are private international investment funds that seek the highest short-term rate of return and invest in the global equity markets including emerging market economies. In this section, each of these is discussed in detail.

The current system was established as a result of the Jamaica Agreement in 1976, which allowed greater flexibility in exchange rates. Previously, under the Bretton Woods System, the foundation of the currency market was a fixed exchange rate regime. In that system, all currencies were fixed against the dollar with exchange rates permitted to move a maximum of 2.25% around the fixed rate. The U.S. dollar was fixed against the price of gold, which was set at $35 per ounce. The advantages of the fixed exchange rate system were that there was currency stability and speculation was discouraged. In the fixed exchange rate system currencies that were not pegged at the correct level against the dollar would experience a balance of payment deficit or surplus. When a country had a deficit, it was necessary to draw on the hard currency reserves of the country to cover the deficit. If the deficit persisted, then the country had to borrow in hard currency in the international market to cover its deficit. In the extreme case of persistence of deficit, the country would seek permission to devalue its currency.

After the Bretton Woods System, a new floating rate system was established enabling the market to determine the exchange rates. Adjustments toward equilibrium in the floating system take place continuously within small increments. There is no need for governments to intervene in the market by drawing on hard currency reserves, or to make fiscal or monetary policy adjustments based on external balances. The G20 countries, a major global economic power, meet to discuss the exchange rates and make sure that the global currency market remains relatively stable. While countries do not normally interfere with the functioning of the market, during times of high turbulence they attempt to stabilize the market through intervention. Major currencies such as the Japanese yen, the euro, the Canadian dollar, and the British pound are free floating against the dollar.

Although the global currency market is viewed as a system of flexible exchange rates, there are a number of countries that have their currency pegged to the U.S. dollar. Therefore, the value of these currencies moves up and down with the U.S. dollar against other major currencies. The most important, and to some degree controversial, is the Chinese Renminbi (RMB or Chinese yuan) parity with the U.S. dollar. This is a particularly controversial issue since China has had a large trade surplus with the United States.

One way to reduce a trade imbalance is by increasing the value of the currency of the country with a trade surplus against the currency of the country with a trade deficit. However, in the case of China, which has a fixed RMB value against the dollar, it is not possible to use the exchange rate as an instrument of adjustment. This issue has created a dispute between the United States and China. While China has increased the value of the RMB against the dollar a number of times, the United States maintains that the currency is still undervalued and further adjustment is necessary.

The International Monetary Fund

The International Monetary Fund (IMF) was established after World War II as part of the Bretton Woods Agreement. The agreement was named after its location: Bretton Woods in the state of New Hampshire, USA. At the conference, representatives of the United States, France, and Britain met and established the foundation of a postwar global financial system. Two institutions were set up to ensure the success of the agreement: the IMF and the International Bank for Reconstruction and Development (IBRD), later known as the World Bank.

The IMF's mandate was and still is the management of the global financial and economic system through the creation of liquidity and the management of the exchange rate system. Initially, the management of the international exchange rate was the main focus of the IMF since the structure of the global financial system was initially based on a fixed exchange rate regime. A fixed exchange rate regime would require that all countries maintain a fixed rate against an anchor currency, which usually is the U.S. dollar. In the Bretton Woods System, the U.S. dollar was the anchor currency and currencies were permitted to fluctuate plus or minus 2.25% against the dollar. Under the fixed exchange rate system, the IMF would provide loans to countries that had a short-term balance of payment deficits and would permit devaluation if they had a structural deficit. However, the fixed exchange rate system eventually collapsed when the United States faced an external deficit and it unilaterally floated the dollar against gold in 1973. In the current system, the role of the IMF has changed to reviewing and recommending economic policy to its member countries rather than getting directly involved in the management of countries' exchange rates.

Another role of the IMF is to provide balance of payment support to its member countries. If a country needed to borrow from the IMF to support their balance of payments, the IMF would insist that the country initiate a structural adjustment of the economy prior to lending the funds. The structural adjustment requirement of the IMF in many cases is viewed as an excessive imposition on the borrowing country. The structural adjustment requirement has raised issues regarding the structural global financial system and has called for readjustment. This is discussed in the latter part of this chapter. But the IMF holds the view that this structural adjustment is required toward creating a healthy and sustainable economic growth for the country and thus for the global economy.

While the function of the IMF has somewhat changed over time, particularly after the breakdown of the fixed exchange rate system, its underlying function of managing the global financial system still remains. The IMF defines its function as:

> The International Monetary Fund (IMF) is an organization of 187 countries, working to foster global monetary cooperation, secure financial stability, facilitate international trade, promote high employment and sustainable economic growth, and reduce poverty around the world. (IMF, 2014)

The IMF has been credited for addressing a number of global financial challenges including the Asian Financial Crisis in 1997 and the Global Financial Crisis of 2008–2010 by preventing the collapse of the international financial system.

The World Bank

The World Bank was originally called the International Bank for Reconstruction and Development (IBRD). It was initially established as an institution to help the economic restructuring of Europe after World War II. In the beginning, funds were provided by the United States to rebuild the infrastructure in Europe after the war. As Europeans paid back their loans with interest, the hard currency reserve of the bank increased. Then the focus turned to helping emerging economies by providing them with project based financing. The World Bank can now raise capital in capital markets at a very low interest rate since it has a AAA rating (World Bank Group, 2014).

The World Bank is essentially a developmental agency. The bank has two major parts: the International Bank for Reconstruction and Development (IBRD) and the International Development Agency (IDA). The IBRD gives loans at market rate interest (including risk premium) to its members for development projects. Projects that are funded by the World Bank must meet both the private rate of return and the social rate of return. They must also be in line with the priorities of the bank. The IDA was established in

1960 and provides low-interest loans (at subsidized rates) to lower-income countries to help with their economic development.

The other institutions of the World Bank are the International Financial Corporation (IFC), the Multilateral Investment Guarantee Agency (MIGA), and the International Center for Settlement of Investments Dispute (ICSID). The IFC's mission is to help the development of the private sectors in developing countries. The MIGA provides political risk insurance for investment in developing countries. The ICSID's primary function is to facilitate conciliation and arbitration of international investment disputes.

International Banks

International banks operate in many different countries. They have a number of different functions including the transfer of funds to private and public sectors, investment in various locations, helping raise capital from one country for another country, and providing information to their clients of market opportunities. They not only facilitate investment, but they also play a key role in international trade financing and managing the fund flow in international trade. Banks are at the core of the integration of the global financial system. International banks can be specifically categorized as follows:

1. **International commercial banks:** These types of banks have overseas branches. They collect deposits and lend to individuals or businesses. International commercial banks also provide trade financing by issuing letters of credit. They have to follow the host country's rules and regulations.
2. **Investment banks:** They are a vehicle for bringing investors and those who require funds together for a fee. They help private sectors or even governments to raise capital by structuring loans and issuing financial instruments. Financial instruments include bonds (government bonds are called sovereign bonds), medium term instruments, and even short-term commercial papers. They underwrite selling shares and bonds for investors. They also invest in overseas financial instruments.
3. **International banks:** International banks play a number of roles depending on their objectives and their mission. At the retail level, they collect deposits and lend locally. In many cases they are also involved in investment banking and in such cases they may not even accept deposits. The business development aspect includes providing information on trade and investment opportuni-

ties and setting up deals for their customers. International banks also put together business deals for their customers across the globe. Most of the deals would require financing that the bank can provide. Many international banks are globalized not only in terms of operations and services, but also in terms of capital structure and even management. Therefore international banks are key institutions for the global economic function including international trade and financial integration, as well as the operation of the global economic system.

The global financial crisis of 2008–2010, however, brought to light both the importance and shortfalls of the international banking system. In particular, it initiated the debate about creating a governance body, or perhaps even an intergovernment organization, that would set the proper governance for global financial institutions.

One such an effort could be based on the Basel Accord for banking supervision. A meeting of central bank officials from around the world in 1988 in Basel, Switzerland, addressed the capital requirements of international banks. This became known as the Basel I Accord issued by the Basel Committee on Banking Supervision. By early 2000 it became clear that Basel I was outdated and that a new set of initiatives would be required. This led to the next round of discussions in 2004 and an agreement that was called Basel II. Basel II raised the capital requirements of banks based on their different types of exposure, provided regulators with greater tools to address systemic risk, and promoted market discipline for risk management. In general, international banks face considerably higher risk in their overseas investments and operations. After the financial crisis, Basel III was created to address the requirement for off-balance-sheet financing of banks and adequacy of capital requirement to match risk exposure (BIS, 2014).

Global Private Investment Funds

Private Investment (PI) funds or hedge funds are an aggregation of capital from a small number of major investors (usually fewer than 100 investors). They are managed by a professional investment organization. These funds are highly aggressive in their approach and seek the highest rate of return during a strong market and reduce losses quickly by exiting the markets during a downturn. Private investment funds are subject to minimal regulation and they do not face the constraint standard investment organizations and mutual funds face.

The global investment funds invest in any company located anywhere in the world including their own country. International funds are similar to global funds, except that international funds cannot invest in their home country.

Global Financial Markets

The main elements of the global financial markets are the foreign exchange market, the international equity market, and the international debt market, which includes loans and bonds. Global financial markets also include a market for complex financial instruments such as swaps, collateralized debt, futures, and options. In this section only, the three main markets are addressed.

Foreign Exchange Market

The foreign exchange market, in its broadest sense, deals with the currency exchange transactions of various countries. The foreign exchange market brings together buyers and sellers of a currency. There are many reasons for currency exchange transactions, for example, the export and import of

TABLE 5.1   Global Foreign Exchange Market Turnover (Net–net basis,[a] daily averages in April, in billions of U.S. dollars)

Instrument	1998	2001	2004	2007	2010	2013
Foreign exchange instruments	1,527	1,239	1,934	3,324	3,971	5,345
Spot transactions	568	386	631	1,005	1,488	2,046
Outright forwards	128	130	209	362	475	680
Foreign exchange swaps	734	656	954	1,714	1,759	2,228
Currency swaps	10	7	21	31	43	54
Options and other products[b]	87	60	119	212	207	337
Memo:						
Turnover at April 2013 exchange rates[c]	1,718	1,500	2,036	3,376	3,969	5,345
Exchange-traded derivatives[d]	11	12	26	80	155	160

[a] Adjusted for local and cross-border inter-dealer double-counting (i.e., "net–net" basis).
[b] The category "other FX products" covers highly leveraged transactions and/or trades whose notional amount is variable and where decomposition into individual plain vanilla components was impractical or impossible.
[c] Non-U.S. dollar legs of foreign currency transactions were converted into original currency amounts at average exchange rates for April of each survey year and then reconverted into U.S. dollar amounts at average April 2013 exchange rates.
[d] *Sources:* FOW TRADEdata; Futures Industry Association; various futures and options exchanges. Foreign exchange futures and options traded worldwide.

goods and services among countries, overseas investments, payment of profit of foreign firms to their parent country, purchase of foreign equity, purchase of foreign bonds, etc. The main players in the currency market are international banks, foreign exchange traders, and central banks of various countries. The most active foreign exchange markets around the globe are in New York, Zurich, Frankfurt, London, Paris, Shanghai, Seoul, Tokyo, and Sydney.

The foreign exchange market includes several financial instruments such as the spot, forward, options, and swap markets as shown on Table 5.1. The reported size of the market by the Bank of International Settlement (BIS) in 2010 was $3,971 billion. Out of that, $1,490 billion was in spot exchanges, $475 billion in forward exchanges, $43 billion in swaps, and $207 billion in options and other transactions (BIS, 2014).

Spot Exchange Rate

The spot exchange rate is the rate one currency is exchanged for a unit of another currency at that instant in time. A currency rate can either be a direct quotation or an indirect quotation against another currency. A direct quotation is the amount of home currency per unit of foreign currency. An indirect quotation is the reverse; it is the amount of foreign currency per unit of home currency. In the case of the dollar, the direct quotation is the amount of dollar per unit of foreign currency. For example, (dollar per euro) is a direct quotation from the U.S. perspective, but a direct quotation in Europe would be (euro per dollar), which is 1 over 1.4. In summary, a direct quotation is the amount of home currency per unit of foreign currency, an indirect quotation is the unit of foreign currency per one unit of home currency.

Transactions in the spot currency market are in the form of bid and offer. A bid is the rate that currency traders buy the currency, and offer is the rate that they sell the currency. The difference between bid and offer is spread. The spread represents two different factors: the transaction cost and the risk factor. The lowest spread is when the transaction takes place in an international bank. The further away from a major bank, for example at the airport, the higher the spread since both transaction cost (the number of times a transaction takes place until it is cleared at the major bank) and risk (the time until the transaction is settled at with a major bank) increase.

A *currency spot transaction* is when the currency exchange takes place at the current moment in time. In the forward market, the transaction will take place sometime in the future, but the rate is set at the current time. Forward rates are set based on the international Fisher effect model that will be discussed later.

Exchange Rate Determination

There are different models to determine exchange rates between various countries. One set of models focuses on the relationship between the balance of trade and the exchange rate, and the competitiveness of the external sector in the world trading system. The second set of models focuses on the relationship between capital flows caused by interest rate differentials of the home country and the foreign countries, and the exchange rate. At the end, both trade and capital flow play a key role in the determination of the exchange rate.

Supply and Demand for Currency

Currency trade takes place for a number of different reasons. Import and export transactions are the most obvious, but there are other reasons including investments in foreign equity markets, foreign direct investment, and even for speculation. Borrowing and lending further creates a need for the foreign exchange market.

The supply and demand approach states that the exchange rate of a country is determined by the supply and demand of goods (including financial) and services from that country. In this model, we assume there is no capital flow. Furthermore, we limit the analysis to two major trading partners: the United States and Europe. The focus is supply and demand for euros, the European currency.

The currency market for the euro and the U.S. dollar is presented in Figure 5.2. In that figure, the supply and demand for the euro are at equilibrium with the exchange rate of Ep at 0.8 euro/$. However, if the euro becomes stronger against the dollar, let's say at 1$ per euro, then U.S. goods become cheaper in Europe and European goods more expensive in the

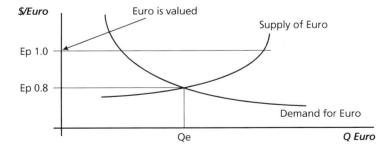

Figure 5.2 Exchange rate determination.

United States. In that case, demand for European goods would drop in the United States and demand for U.S. products would increase in Europe. At this point, Ep 1.0, there is a balance of trade deficit in Europe and a surplus in the United States. The system then has to get to a balanced structure. Under the fixed system (before 1972) the governments of European countries would have to sell US$ and buy euros to balance the trade deficit. In the flexible exchange rate system, balance is achieved by market forces. Therefore, if there is demand for a currency, the price of the currency will be higher. This will lead the system toward an equilibrium rate of 0.8 dollar per euro that implies that the euro has become weaker and the dollar stronger. In sum, the exchange rate is determined by the purchasing power of currency in relation to the currency of the trading partners.

The question is what changes the purchasing power of one currency against another? The main factor that leads to change in the exchange rate between two countries is the competitiveness of the price of goods as a result of a change in their prices, according to relative purchasing power parity. In other words, the changes in the competitiveness reflect the differences in the inflation rate of the countries involved.

Capital Flow

Capital flow between countries also impacts their exchange rate. The Fisher effect and the international Fisher effect are two models that explain the relation between capital movement among countries and the exchange rate. The Fisher effect model shows the relationship between the interest rate, inflation, and capital flow. When all the variables remain constant, any increase in the nominal interest rate will lead to a capital inflow. The international Fisher effect model focuses on the relation between interest rates and exchange rates. It argues that if the interest rate increases in a country, to avoid capital flow the exchange rate must go down.

Complete Exchange Rate Model

Exchange rate forecasting is an art. While the main factors impacting future exchange rates were discussed in the previous section, there are other factors that impact future exchange rates. Factors such as political risk and excessive balance of payment deficit cause major changes in the forecast of economic activities and also impact the exchange rate. In a period of political crisis the exchange rate normally falls. Historically, the U.S. dollar was viewed as a safe refuge for international capital during the global crisis. However, the emergence of the euro as competitive currency could change the picture and it could also be used as safe store of value during an international political crisis period.

Finally, a large balance of payment deficit, as was explained previously, could lead to currency devaluation. It should be noted that while in a floating system this disequilibrium is corrected by exchange rate adjustments, in a managed exchange rate system, it requires government drawing on their foreign currency.

We can see that the integration of only two subsystems can create a complex system that is beyond the human capability to intuitively understand the effect of changing one factor to the whole system. Therefore, many intuitive solutions may not create an expected outcome.

The Forward Market

As was mentioned earlier, there are a number of other currency markets known as derivatives. One such a market is the forward currency market. The forward currency rate is a rate that is quoted by a bank or other financial institutions for a transaction in the future. The forward market is custom made according to the amount and the date of the transaction. The quotation in the forward market is in terms of bid and offer. The bid is the rate that the currency is bought and the offer rate is the rate that the currency is sold. The difference between the bid and the offer is called spread. The spread increases as the length of the contract into the future increases. For example, the spread for a 6-month forward market is greater than the spread for 1 month.

The forward market is used to hedge the currency risk. In the case of a foreign currency receivable, selling in the forward market at a fixed rate eliminates the foreign exchange risk. In the case of payables, the firm can buy foreign currency at a fixed forward rate to eliminate foreign exchange risk. The cost of hedging the currency risk in a forward market can be treated as a business expense to eliminate risk, in the same way that a firm buys insurance against risk.

One drawback of using the forward market is that if a transaction is fixed, if at maturity the exchange rate is in our favor, we must still honor the deal. In other words, while hedging in the forward market eliminates exchange rate risk, it also eliminates the potential of foreign exchange gain. But, leaving the exchange rate unhedged in hopes of a foreign currency gain makes the firm in essence a speculator on the foreign exchange market. Since currency speculation is not a core competency of firms involved in international trade and investment, then it is highly recommended that they eliminate the risk by covering their foreign exchange exposure.

The forward rate is determined by the international Fisher effect model. The value of the forward rate should be equal to the spot rate multiplied by the interest rate differential between the home market and foreign market. If this condition does not hold, then there is the potential for arbitrage between the spot-currency market and the money market.

The Global Equity Market

Most countries around the world have stock markets where stock of various companies is traded in their own currencies. These equity markets have blossomed after emerging economies changed toward a more open and free market. The stock markets of transition economies in particular have expanded as a result of privatization of state owned companies. Developed economies have had their equity markets functioning for many years and are well established. But the development of equity markets in emerging economies is a relatively new phenomenon. One of the main characteristics of the equity markets is that they do not generally discriminate based on whether the fund is a domestic or foreign investment. This openness of the equity markets has benefited both overseas investors who are looking for the highest rate of return and the domestic companies that are searching for liquidity.

Another benefit of international investment for investors is the ability to diversify their risk. Risk diversification is based on the principle that country specific risk varies among nations. By investing funds in various countries, the risk of investment is spread around and it is reduced. The lower correlation between equity markets in which the investment takes place, the greater is the risk diversification.

Two main factors that impact the risk of international portfolio investment are the correlation of the equity market among various countries and the second is the exchange rate fluctuation between the countries. The more correlated the movement of the stock markets of two countries, the lower the risk diversification of investment. Also, the more volatile the exchange rate between the two countries, the higher the risk of the portfolio in dollar terms, assuming that the dollar is the home currency.

Increasingly various stock markets across the globe are becoming integrated due to cross listing as well as general economic and business linkages across the globe. Cross listing occurs when a firm lists its stock in a country other than the home country. Cross listing is particularly attractive for companies from small countries with a limited capital base that are trying to raise funds in the United States. In that case, they offer their shares in U.S. dollars in the New York Stock Exchange (NYSE) in the form of American depository receipts (ADRs). ADRs are the price of the stock (or a multiple of the price) in U.S. dollars. Therefore if the stock price changes either in the home country or in the United States, or if the exchange rate changes, through arbitrage (buying in one market and selling simultaneously in the other market) the value becomes the same.[1]

The Global Debt Market

The global debt market provides a variety of financing instruments with different options regarding maturity, payment structure, and currencies. The main sources of debt financing are international bank loans, syndicated loans, the international bond market, and the euro market.

International banks have historically been a source of funds for local firms outside their country. Borrowing dollars outside of the United States (called euro dollars) has the benefit of obtaining a lower interest rate on a loan than a dollar loan in the United States. This is because the euro dollar market is unregulated and is a wholesale market.

Euro dollar credit is usually given to institutions or to the governments (called sovereign credit) by the banks in U.S. dollar terms. Normally, the credit is pegged to the LIBOR (London Interbank Offer Rate). The LIBOR is the borrowing rate in London among banks. It is used as the benchmark for lending and borrowing internationally. Normally borrowing is in the form of LIBOR plus certain points. The points reflect the risk associated with that specific borrowing.

A syndicated loan is similar to a bank loan, but it includes a group of banks that partner in lending. This is particularly the case for large loans when a bank does not want to be highly exposed to such a loan. A syndicated loan is usually organized by a bank called the lead bank. In turn, the lead bank markets the loan to a small number of international banks. There is also a management bank. The management bank's function is to collect interest and to distribute it to member banks based on their participation. The management bank in essence acts as the representative of all the other banks participating in the financing of the credit.

Impact of the Global Financial System

The global financial system has provided a working structure that has led to a relatively high economic growth for a number of countries and specifically has helped to fuel the growth of many emerging economies. It has led to the movement of capital resources from countries with excessive capital with low marginal productivity to countries with limited capital where marginal capital productivity was high. Yet the system has its own critics and there are those who call for the reforming of the global financial system (Stiglitz, 2007).

The current criticism of the financial system is based on a number of different factors. One of the criticisms is that due to the integration of the system, the financial problems of each country will have global implications that are transferred to other countries. This is particularly true for countries that are economically and financially strong. A financial problem in one of these countries can be globalized and have such an impact that it could potentially lead to the collapse of the global financial system. Stiglitz argues that a global financial crisis has become the norm rather than an occasional occurrence (Stiglitz, 2003).

In the last two decades, there have been numerous crises such as the Mexican peso crisis in 1995, the Asian financial crisis in 1997, the Russian crisis in 1998, the Argentina financial crisis in 2002, the U.S. financial crisis in 2008, and most recently the Greek financial crisis in 2010. These are a few of the well-known crises that have occurred and have had a global impact. Each crisis had its unique causes, but their impact affected many different countries. The U.S. financial crisis almost resulted in the collapse of the whole system.

The second set of criticisms is based on the fairness of the structure of the global financial system. One of the most outspoken critics of the system is Joseph Stiglitz, a noted economist who has argued that a well-functioning system will shift funds from capital rich developed countries to poor countries. But the current system has led the flow of funds to go from emerging economies to developed countries including the United States (Stiglitz, 2003). Secondly, even when there is capital flow to the developing countries, it is not going to the countries that are most in need of global financial resources, such as Sub-Saharan Africa.

However, the defenders of the system argue that the problem is partially due to the governance and legal institutions in those countries. It is argued that improvements in the governance and legal systems to protect investments would lead to an increase in capital flow, further resulting in higher economic growth and an improvement in economic well-being, which in turn would further increase the capital flow.

The third set of criticisms is that capital flows across geographical boundaries, particularly in the equity market, have become highly short term and speculative. This has created an inherent destabilization of the global financial market. In other words, excessive capital flow creates an artificial liquidity that fuels fast economic growth. However, once there are signs of economic problems, then there is a quick capital outflow. Therefore, the system has a built-in destabilizing element (Bhagwati, 1998).

However, others argue that the system has managed to address each crisis and has sustained itself. They argue that if it was not for the current system, the world's economy would have collapsed. They also argue that while the system has not helped every country to move out of poverty, it has been instrumental in shifting many of the low-income countries toward becoming middle income level. Supporters admit that there are some shortcomings, particularly in regards to modern financial instruments. But any adjustment must be in the form of fine-tuning and not a complete change of the system.

Joseph Stiglitz in his critique of the current global system has put forward a number of ideas for reforming the global financial system. One idea proposed by Stiglitz was a new global reserve system. He also suggested that international financial institutions such as the IMF must become more democratic and more sensitive toward the needs of the least developed countries. His suggestion is that the "global greenback" can be managed by the International Monetary Fund in a similar manner as the special drawing rights (SDRs) if the IMF is reformed. Obviously the concept of global currency faces strong opposition from the United States and has not emerged in any way as a practical option to the U.S. dollar.

Parity Condition

Purchasing Power Parity (PPP)

Absolute

Under absolute PPP, the exchange rate between two currencies is equal to the price ratio of the products.

$$E = Ph/Pi$$

This approach assumes that there are only two countries and only two products. The price of each product represents the average price in each country. Some economists compare the price of a Big Mac in various countries to determine whether a currency is overpriced or not (see Table 5.2). The Big Mac is a convenient product since it is sold in 120 countries. The theory is that the Big Mac should cost the same in each location (see Figure 5.3). The Big Mac costs about $3 in the United States.

TABLE 5.2   Exchange Rate Calculation Based on the Big Mac Index

Country Currency		Big Mac Price	Exchange Rate[*]	Comments
Indonesian Rupiah	IDR	4000	1$ = 9,205.50	Out of Balance[**]
Columbian Peso	COP	2,360.5	1$ = 2,600	Out of Balance[**]
Taiwan Dollar	TWD	100	1$ = 33.220	About Right
Jordanian Dinar	JOD	1	1$ = 0.7085	Out of Balance[**]

[*] Exchange Rate as of October 13, 2006
[**] Out of balance, dollar is overvalued

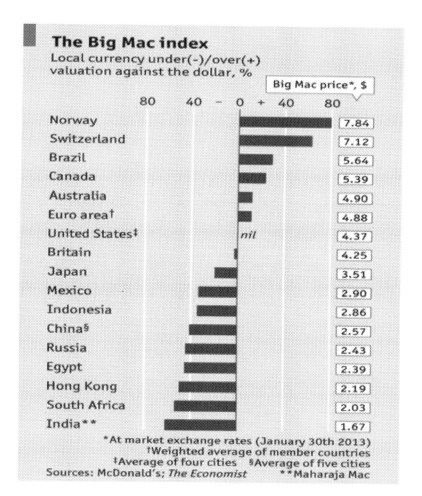

Figure 5.3 2013 Big Mac Index result. *Source:* http://www.economist.com/
content/big-mac-index/

This does not take into consideration other factors that affect the price, such as the price of rent, insurance, profit margins, taxes, or transportation costs that vary from country to country. In reality, this is probably a better indicator of the relative size of the economy as opposed to the market exchange rate.

Relative Purchasing Power Parity

Relative PPP argues that the exchange rate between two countries is a function of the inflation rate between the two countries. It is assumed that the exchange rate between the two countries is at equilibrium. To remain at equilibrium, the exchange rate change must be equal and opposite to the inflation rate differential between the two countries (see Figure 5.4).

The line that divides the right angle into two (i.e., 45 degrees) is the equilibrium line and shows the equilibrium relation between the inflation rate differential and the need for exchange rate devaluation or revaluation. That is any point on the horizontal axis (shows the inflation rate differential), through the 45-degree line, is transferred to the vertical axis (shows the needed exchange rate adjustment). What happens if transformation does not take place through the equilibrium line? In that case the currency will either be overvalued or undervalued.

The Indonesian rupiah trades at about 9,000/$1 (rounded off in this example).

Inflation rate of Indonesia is about 20%.
Inflation rate in the U.S. is about 4%.

$$e_t = 9000 \ (1 + 0.2) / (1 + 0.04)$$
$$e_t = 10{,}385$$

Future exchange rate should reach about 11,000.

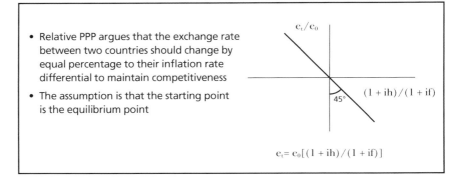

- Relative PPP argues that the exchange rate between two countries should change by equal percentage to their inflation rate differential to maintain competitiveness
- The assumption is that the starting point is the equilibrium point

e_t / e_0

$(1 + ih) / (1 + if)$

45°

$e_t = e_0 [(1 + ih) / (1 + if)]$

Figure 5.4 Relative purchasing power parity.

Another less precise way to approximate this is:

$$(ih - if) = 20 - 4\% = 16\% \text{ approximate \% increase so,}$$
$$1.16 \ (9,000) = 10,440$$

How accurately does PPP forecast value of exchange rate? Empirical studies have determined that in the long run and when the inflation rate differentials are high, PPP is a good estimator of a future exchange rate. However, it is not a good predictor for a short-term forecast or when the inflation rate differential is small. This is because there are other random factors that impact the value of the future exchange rate that could be more significant than the inflation rate differential.

The Fisher Effect

This approach is based upon the principle that money will flow to the country where it will earn the highest real rate of return (interest rate adjusted for inflation). The model claims that if two countries start at equilibrium and the objective is not to have capital flow between the countries, then the interest rate differential must be equal to the inflation rate differential between the two countries. In other words, the real interest rate has to be the same in order to prevent capital flow between the two countries.

To illustrate this, we will use Canada (home), and the United States (foreign).

> Inflation rate in Canada (ih) is 6%.
> Interest rate in the U.S. (rf) is 6%.
> Inflation in the U.S. (if) is 4%.

So, rh = $[1.06 \ (1.06/1.04)] - 1 = 0.08$ or 8%.

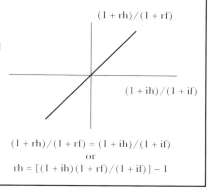

- In order to prevent capital flow between two countries, the interest rate differential must be exactly equal to the inflation rate differential between the two

- The assumption is that there is an equilibrium in the market

$(1 + rh)/(1 + rf)$

$(1 + ih)/(1 + if)$

$(1 + rh)/(1 + rf) = (1 + ih)/(1 + if)$
or
$rh = [(1 + ih)(1 + rf)/(1 + if)] - 1$

Figure 5.5 Fisher effect.

Therefore, if the interest rate in Canada is less than 8%, then capital will flow into the United States. One of the assumptions of the Fisher effect is that the investment risk in both countries is the same. Clearly if the investment risk in a country is high even if the real interest rate is marginally higher, it would not lead to capital flow. In fact, one can observe that there is usually capital flight from countries with political risk to other more politically stable countries, even if the interest rate differential remains in favor of the former.

The International Fisher Effect

The international Fisher effect simplifies the Fisher effect by considering the interest rates instead of a combination of the interest rates and the inflation rates (see Figure 5.6). The international Fisher effect argues that if the exchange rate change must be equal and opposite to that of the inflation rate differential and the interest rate differential must be equal to the inflation rate differential, then the exchange rate change must be equal and opposite to the interest rate differential.

Notice that this is similar to Relative PPP, only the interest rate is used in this evaluation instead of the inflation rate.

Conclusion

Global trade and investment has brought the world closer and has created an integrated system of economic interdependency between various countries. The main benefit has been a period of relatively high economic growth and the emergence and transformation of a number of developing

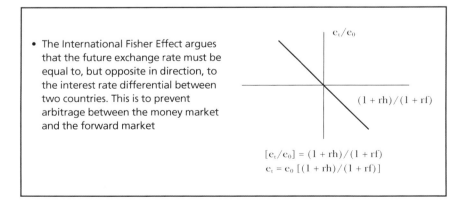

- The International Fisher Effect argues that the future exchange rate must be equal to, but opposite in direction, to the interest rate differential between two countries. This is to prevent arbitrage between the money market and the forward market

e_t/e_0

$(1 + rh)/(1 + rf)$

$$[e_t/e_0] = (1 + rh)/(1 + rf)$$
$$e_t = e_0\,[(1 + rh)/(1 + rf)]$$

Figure 5.6 International Fisher effect.

countries through this system toward developed economies. Examples of this phenomenon include China, India, South Korea, and Brazil. However, at the same time it has created a system of risk transfer particularly from major economies toward smaller economies. The system withstood pressure during the Asian financial crisis of 1997–1999. But the economic and financial crisis of 2008 in the United States was globalized and impacted a number of its partners in trade and the financial system. In other words, while we have a global financial and economic system, the systemic risk has also internationalized.

Note

1. For further discussion of ADRs see Eiteman, Stonehill, and Moffett, Multinational Business Finance, 10th edition Pages 328–331. Eiteman, David, S. A. (2004). *Multinational Business Finance,* Boston, MA: Pearson Addison Wesley.

SECTION II

Firm Level International Business

6

International Business Strategy

This chapter explains the process of strategic planning. Various dynamic aspects of international strategy are integrated to describe the development of international business strategy within the context of the overall business strategy of a firm. Finally, applications of the tripod model are discussed.

Strategy is a roadmap for the future of an organization. It provides guidance for various stakeholders including investors, management, and other people working in the organization. In essence, strategy sets the vision for the future of the enterprise and the objectives of the organization along with guidance on how they will be achieved. The main goal of a firm is value creation for the owners, both in the short term and in the long run, while taking into account the interest of other stakeholders and society. For state-owned enterprises (SOEs), the main objective is the creation of both social benefits and private benefits, such as job creation and financial returns.

Strategy formulation is a complex process and requires building a vision for the future of the organization, evaluating the firm's core competence, identifying the external environment in terms of opportunities and threats, developing an action plan, and continuously evaluating progress

Foundations of Global Business, pages 89–99
Copyright © 2016 by Information Age Publishing
All rights of reproduction in any form reserved.

89

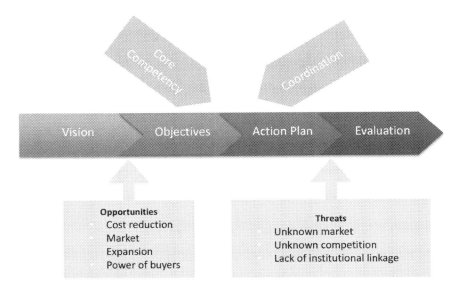

Figure 6.1 Strategic planning elements.

(see Figure 6.1). Appropriate implementation not only requires analysis and the development of an action plan, but it also requires effective execution. An effective execution alone may need a number of factors and processes that take into account changes in the culture of the organization, leadership, reorganization, and reallocation of resources.

Strategy must have at least two clear and identifiable sets of objectives: financial and strategic. The financial objectives analyze the financial situation of the firm and the ways it can be improved. Normally, financial performances such as the return on investment (ROI) and the return on assets (ROA) are benchmarked against industry averages to show how well the firm is performing financially. Improvement in financial performance and profitability can be achieved by increasing sales, cutting costs, or a combination of both. An increase in sales can come from an aggressive domestic market expansion via the introduction of new products, marketing efforts, upgrades in the technology used, and new design. Cost rationalization would focus on a more efficient use of resources.

Regarding market expansion, another option is to expand into new markets internationally. The cost-cutting approach of international expansion focuses on analyzing the value chain to determine which part or parts of the value chain of the firm can operate more efficiently through the use of technology, relocation to lower cost countries, outsourcing, and offshoring (Hamel, 1991; Hamel & Prahalad, 1985).

One way that firms can reduce costs is to move their production site to places with lower cost resources, particularly labor, such as China and India. In the manufacturing sector, offshoring has become a way to reduce the cost of production. To increase revenue, firms need to tap into new markets in order to expand the market size. Both methods increase a firm's profit, which pushes the target profit even higher. Market expansion internationally leads to higher revenue, which increases the profit of the company.

The main strategic objective focuses on determining the long-term positioning of the firm relative to its competitors. Competing for market share may have certain incremental costs in the short term, such as investment in research and development (R&D), which takes years before it yields new products or technology. However, without investment in R&D, the firm would be leveraging its future for saving costs in the short term. Such a strategy would not be sustainable and would be detrimental to the firm's long-term success and well-being.

Analytical Approach: Tripod Strategy

One strategic planning model is the tripod model of strategy formulation (see Figure 6.2). The tripod model proposes that strategy must be approached from three dimensions: the resource-based view (RBV), the industry-based view, and the institution-based view (Peng, 2013).

The resource-based view focuses on the internal resources that the firm has that differentiate it from its competitors. Some of the resources are tangible assets, such as financial resources, plants and equipment, and technology, while some other assets are intangible such as management capabilities and name recognition. One can argue that intangible assets are as important as tangible assets in building firm level competitive advantage. Both tangible

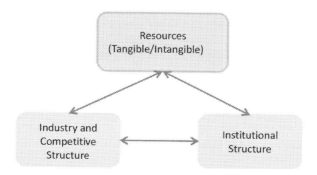

Figure 6.2 Strategy formulation approach.

and intangible assets are accumulated over time. While tangible assets are easy to see and their accumulation over time is recognizable, the intangible assets are more difficult to recognize. Over time their accumulation would provide a competitive advantage for the firm and would differentiate it from its competitors (Peng, 2001, 2002; Peng, Wang, & Jiang, 2008).

The industry-based view focuses on the external factors that impact the operation of the firm within a particular industry. This includes the stage of industry life cycle, the dynamic changes of industry (DCI), and the competitive nature of the industry. The industry analysis also requires evaluation of the competitive structure of the industry including the number of competitors. The degree of industry concentration is an important dimension of the competitive structure of an industry. When there are large numbers of firms within an industry and products are not differentiated, there is much less competition within the industry in terms of marketing. Going international when an industry has reached its maturity stage with a lower growth rate may provide an opportunity for increasing sales.

The institution-based view focuses on the institutional aspect in the process of strategy formulation. The institutional aspect includes government regulation and legal aspects. The institution-based view also looks at the silent aspect of institutions that include culture, social norms, and social values. A new government regulation at home may make the operation more difficult and could pressure the profit margin of the firm. Similarly, pressure could arise from social norms and changes in the value system pushing the firm to look internationally. An example is the institutional pressure on the U.S. tobacco industry since the early 1980s. The U.S. government began regulating this industry due to health concerns as well as an increase in healthcare costs related to cigarette smoking. The public also began campaigning against smoking in the United States, leading to a change in the attitude toward smoking in the country. In order to maintain their profit margin, a number of tobacco companies shifted their focus to international markets, particularly in developing countries where the anti-smoking culture had not yet developed and where government regulations and the legal system were less negative against tobacco companies.

Tripod Model Extended

The tripod model can be further expanded to add two more dimensions (see Figure 6.3). These are the dynamic capability and the system base view. By dynamic capability we imply the ability of an enterprise to build assets, both tangible and intangible, for future growth as well as the ability to be nimble and make necessary adjustments to external changes.

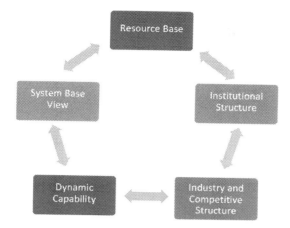

Figure 6.3 Tripod model diagram.

International strategy is particularly important in this regard because of the dynamic and continuously changing global business environment.

The system view, as discussed earlier, requires an understanding of the strategy implications on other parts of the enterprise and the external system. It also implies the ability to internalize changes in the external system to the firm level system. For example, a firm's strategy of international expansion impacts its risk. Diversification of operations and sales avoids the risk of dependency on only one location and one market. But it also creates incremental risk due to the country specific risk of a new location. In particular, if the strategy requires financial investment in terms of foreign direct investment, requiring additional capital could increase the cost of capital of the firm.

International Business Strategy: 5 W Model

International strategy focuses on how a firm benefits from internationalization in achieving its objectives. A firm can have multiple objectives including increasing sales, lowering cost, increasing its competitive position, or acquiring knowledge through internationalization. The international strategy of a firm must focus on achieving those objectives by exploring the potential in other countries. Market expansion is one of the important motivations for the internationalization of a firm. The international market and, in particular, emerging economies with their increasing per capita income and a large population, provide an incredible market potential. China and India together have a population of approximately 2.4 billion

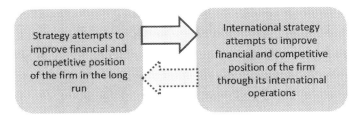

Figure 6.4 Fit between general strategy and international strategy.

people. While their per capita income is relatively low, in the last decade their rate of growth has been three times that of most developed Western countries. This has provided a great opportunity for companies that are interested in increasing their sales and their revenue. This was particularly important during the economic recession of 2008–2010.

Firms also go international in order not to lose sales if their customers are moved overseas. For example, in the 1980s when a number of Japanese car manufacturers (Toyota and Honda) moved their production facilities to the United States, the tire producer Bridgestone realized that in order to remain close to its major customers, it had to set up operations in the United States to continue serving Toyota and Honda. Thus Bridgestone acquired Firestone.

Reducing cost is another potential reason for MNEs to look into operating internationally. Many companies have set up offshore activities to take advantage of cheaper labor costs overseas. The cost differential along with the lower overhead requirements for operating in a number of developing countries, particularly in China, have been the driving force for many companies currently operating there. Another approach for international cost reduction is the business process of outsourcing. Particularly outsourcing services and the operational side of certain activities in order to reduce costs has become the norm. India is among the many attractive locations for outsourcing activities. The country is well positioned for those activities due to its large English speaking and well-educated population. Many companies have outsourced back-office activities such as accounting, payroll, and document maintenance as well as customer service to India. This has reduced their cost significantly because of the labor cost differential between the United States and India.

The international business strategy of a firm must address four main questions called the 5Ws of international business strategy (see Figure 6.5):

1. Why is a firm going international? This is the key question to be asked by the firm. Much of the subsequent decisions are based on

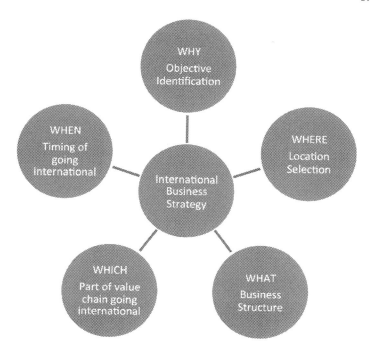

Figure 6.5 5Ws of international strategy.

the answer to this question. The main reasons, as was explained previously, are: (1) increase in revenue, (2) reduction in cost, (3) risk diversification, and (4) a combination of these factors.

2. Which activities will go abroad? The firm needs to do a value chain analysis to ensure that the international strategy fits well with its overall competitive strategy. Value chain analysis requires the disaggregation of activities to its components. Once this is done, the firm then must decide which activities should move overseas and which ones should be kept domestic.

3. What is the best ownership structure? The decision as to whether a firm would use its financial resources or would rather limit its international financial exposure is a key decision. In other words, it is crucial to determine the mode of entry and operation. Various options would include export, strategic alliance, licensing, joint venture, and wholly owned subsidiary. These will be discussed in detail in later chapters.

4. Where should the various activities be located? Location selection is an important strategic decision particularly in international

business strategy. Each foreign location offers certain advantages such as market potential or cost advantage. At the same time, a number of issues such as cultural differences, risk factors, availability of infrastructure, and government regulations are a few of the factors that must be taken into account for location selection.

5. When relates to the timing of expanding to a new country. When entering into a new location, a firm must ask the following question: Should we enter now or wait to enter later? Waiting would provide additional information and time for evaluating the risk. This is particularly valuable for high-risk locations. The *wait and see* strategy is also important for countries that are in temporary economic or political turmoil. However, waiting involves additional cost. The cost of delay could potentially be a lost opportunity. In many cases it is important for a firm to seize a strategic opportunity since a delay would have an opportunity cost. Therefore, firms must compare the benefits of delay and the associated cost. A cost benefit analysis of a strategy is the answer to when. Other more technical models of strategy evaluation (such as the "Real Option") exist, but these models are not the focus of this book and can be accessed in relevant literature.

Those decisions are important and should take into account resources that are available to the firm. But the competitive structure of industry and institutional aspects of countries should also be taken into account.

Topology of Operational Strategies

While in a broad sense firms develop an international strategy, the form of the strategy is different depending on the industry structure, the need for local responsiveness, and the requirements for international integration. In general, there are three potential approaches that a firm can adopt in its operation strategy. They are a global strategy, a multidomestic strategy, and an international strategy. Each of these strategies is briefly discussed below.

1. Global strategy focuses on viewing the world as one market. A global strategy works best when there is very little need to make adjustments for local needs and when a firm meets the same competitors in various countries. The advantage of a global strategy is that the firm is able to reduce its cost structure by standardization in various markets and to compete effectively on a cost and price basis through the achievement of economies of scale.

2. Multidomestic strategy is the opposite of a global strategy. When the need to adjust to local requirements including cultural aspects and competitive structure is high, there is not much benefit in standardization to achieve economies of scale. In this situation, competition is highly localized and therefore the competitive strategy must be built around the local attributes. In such cases, firms provide a great deal of flexibility to local management to make the necessary changes in product, services and the strategy in general to improve the competitive position in that country or location.

3. International strategy is when the firm needs to make some adjustments to its core competency to improve its local competitiveness. It is a strategy that represents a middle ground between a global strategy and a multidomestic strategy. In an international strategy, a firm determines its country specific strategy based on the core competencies. Core competencies such as technology, brand recognition, and management capability are the basis of the strategy. However, the difference between an international strategy and a global strategy is that the local managers have some flexibility to make adjustments to improve the operations in each location. In addition, usually there is feedback from the headquarters.

Over time the firms may change their approach based on the circumstances and their accumulation of experience. A firm may initially begin with a global strategy and change it later to a multidomestic strategy when management realizes that in a particular market it is difficult to compete

Figure 6.6   Elements of strategy.

unless they make certain adjustments based on local needs. Many fast-food companies who entered China started with a fixed menu but adjusted over time to the needs of local taste.

Sometimes a firm enters a new market using the home-country functional strategy, such as marketing or financial strategy, but later adjusts it as needed to increase competitiveness. As the firm accumulates knowledge and understanding, it is able to further expand internationally. Learning experience and knowledge accumulation is an intangible asset that further helps the internationalization of the firm by improving its competitive position in the global marketplace.

Based on its understanding of global industry and competitive structure, the firm would need to adopt one of the above approaches. However, there are cases in which a firm may use a mixed strategy for its various products or divisions. A firm could have a global strategy for some of its products, a multinational for others, and adopt an international strategy for yet another segment of its products.

Internalization Theory

Buckley and Casson (1998) used a broad-based intellectual framework based on the original work of Ronald Coase to analyze multinational operation aspects such as technology transfer, international trade, and location in relation to internationalization strategies. The combined effects of location and internalization strategies explained the division in certain markets between domestic producers, local subsidiaries of MNEs, exports from foreign-owned plants, and exports from MNEs. Internalization is a general principle that explains the boundaries of organizations. It applies not only to the geographical boundaries of the firm, but also to other boundaries such as the firm's product range or diversification. By using this approach, the multinational firm was viewed as a complex system of interdependent activities linked by flows of knowledge and intermediate products (Buckley & Casson, 1998, 2009; Buckley & Ghauri, 2004; Coase, 1937).

This view of the multinational firm was a radical departure from the neoclassical economic view of the firm as a unitary black box devoted entirely to production, whose inputs and outputs were related by a simple production function. The new vision of the firm emphasized the internal division of labor, involving specialized functions comprising not only production but also marketing and R&D. The power of the internalization concept was such that it was believed that using a global system view would make it possible to analyze a very wide range of practical issues in international business. Two distinct forms of internalization were identified: operational internalization, involving intermediate products flowing through successive stages of production and the distribution channel and knowledge internalization or the internalization of the flow of knowledge emanating from R&D. The gains from R&D internalization can be substantial and they stem from asymmetric information (Hamel, 1991).

7

Location Selection

This chapter describes the location selection process. Measureable indicators of location selection are discussed, as well as the relationship between the location's institutions and the firm. The role of clusters in selecting a location is also described.

The location selection is a critical aspect of international business strategy. Although many believe that information and communications technology has made distance less relevant in the way we do business still today, location matters particularly in international business operations. Location specific institutional factors such as government regulations, cultural factors, and preferences as well as economic elements including nontransferable resources require careful analysis of where certain activities of the firm should take place in order to build and sustain competitive advantage. Proper location selection provides a firm with a distinct advantage (Cairncross, 2001; Dunning, 2009).

The question is whether firms look globally or into a specific region when making their location selection. It is argued that the activities of multinationals have become increasingly regionalized. The three major

Foundations of Global Business, pages 101–116
Copyright © 2016 by Information Age Publishing

regions, NAFTA, the European Union, and Asia are the main focus of MNE activity. Rugman and Verbeke (2004) found that for a sample of 320 of the largest firms, more than 80% of their sales are concentrated in the triad (USA, Japan, and EU). They maintain that this supports the regionalization argument as opposed to the globalization one. The regionalization argument is re-enforced by the psychic distance hypothesis (Rugman & Verbeke, 2004).

A great deal of research on psychic distance was built around the work of Swedish researchers Johanson and Vahlne (1977) and Johanson and Wiedersheim-Paul (1975). The psychic distance hypothesis maintains that MNEs prefer to do business, at least initially, with countries that are fairly similar to their home country. Psychic distance includes factors such as cultural similarity, language, business norms, education level, and similarity of economic development as well as physical distance. In such situations firms feel they are familiar with the business environment and are capable of assessing business risk properly (Johanson & Vahlne, 1977; Johanson & Wiedersheim-Paul, 1975).

The psychic distance theory, however, presents a different aspect of internationalization than the standard theory of comparative advantage. The comparative advantage theory contends that the greatest gain from international activities comes from doing business with countries that have a different endowment of factors of production. Psychic distance theory maintains that there is a greater business relation with similar countries. The way to reconcile the two is that the former emphasizes the cost and supply side, while the latter highlights the demand side as the main driver of international business. The components of the psychic distance can be physical distance, cultural distance, and language. These are the cultural and geographic dimensions of Ghemawat's framework (Ghemawat, 2001; Ricart, Enright, Ghemawat, Hart, & Khanna, 2004). The physical distance can be seen as proxy for transportation costs, traffic, and other nontariff barriers.

It is important to consider separately the companies that are trying to select a location for the first time from the ones that are already operating internationally and are interested in either expanding or reducing their operations in a particular country. In the first case, the firm lacks the proper information to assess locational attractiveness and the risk. In the second case, the firm not only has information about the location, but it also is able to assess its own competitive situation of the location and therefore make an informed decision.

Choice of Location for Expansion

Country selection requires the consideration of a number of different and complex factors. Among the important factors to be considered is the ability of the firm to coordinate activities across the network of operation. It does require coordination between headquarters and other locations as well as various locations overseas. This requires the analysis of a number of issues such as logistics, management and operational aspects, quality control, and after sale services. The need for control varies depending on the firm's operational strategy. A standardization strategy (global strategy) would need tight control and monitoring of the international operations to assure consistency and cost control, whereas localization strategy (multi-domestic strategy) would need less coordination among different locations.

The institutional factors, both explicit and implicit, are also important for the selection of location. The local rules and regulations, the structure of corporate governance, the tax structure, and the local attitude toward foreign firms are all important decision points.

In the case of initial entry, a firm must evaluate all the alternatives and not solely focus on a single location. Scanning and assessing different options for strategic fit between the location and aim of its internationalization

LOCATION SPECIFIC FACTORS

Ability to coordinate locational activities
- Between headquarter and overseas locations
- Among various overseas locations

Institutional factors
- Local rules and regulations
- Attitude toward foreign companies (liability of foreignness)
- Cultural differences
- Structure of corporate governance

Location specific risk
- Political risk
- Economic risk
- Competitive risk
- Exchange rate risk

Attractiveness of Business Environment
- Cost structure (for resources seekers)
- Purchasing power
- Economic growth

is crucial. It is also critical to collect relevant data and analyze quantitatively such a fit.

Previously we noted that the internationalization objective of a firm could be seeking new markets to increase sales, to obtain natural resources, to access cheap labor, to diversify the risk of dependence on one or a limited number of countries, or to improve their competitive position. Depending on a firm's objective, the focus will be on different parameters depicting the country's attractiveness for its operation.

For example, a market seeker tends to look for locations that have a high purchasing power and are relatively robust in terms of economic growth. Whereas a firm that is seeking cheap labor focuses on wages and salaries and their potential increase due to inflation. For such firms, the availability of natural resources would not be an important factor. However, for a natural resources seeking firm, such as an oil company, looking for additional international oil reserves is important. An international oil company in choosing a location must consider oil reserves, infrastructure for exploration, potential export facilities, as well as political and other risks of investment. For an oil company the location issue is less relevant than economic growth.

Another example is a firm that internationalizes to diversify its risk. Such a firm would need to analyze the degree of economic and financial integration of the new location with the home country. The more closely the two countries are related, the less risk diversification occurs for the firm when establishing operations in the foreign country. For risk diversification, other economic factors are less important. Table 7.1 shows the different factors a firm would consider depending on its main internationalization objective. The horizontal axis shows the objective and the vertical axis is the location attribute that a firm could be considering. Purchasing power is important for market seekers but not for resource seekers nor for risk diversifiers. However, labor cost is important for a firm that is looking for inexpensive labor in its international strategy, but not important for market seekers or firms that are looking for natural resources. It is also somewhat important for those firms that look for a competitive advantage. If they manage to bring the cost down without competitors following their strategy, they may build advantage. If competitors follow them, then the advantage may be only temporary.

It is possible to quantify and rank various country factors on a scale from 1 to 10 (1 = low and 10 = high). In order to quantify the various factors important for the firm's internationalization, they must be listed. For some of these factors quantitative data are available. Factors such as economic growth,

TABLE 7.1 Location Selection Factors

	Market Seeker	Resource Seeker		Risk Diversifier	Competitive Positioning
		Natural resources	Cheap labor		
Purchasing Power	Important	Not important	Not important	Not important	Somewhat important
Economic Growth	Important	Not important	Not important	Somewhat important	Somewhat important
Inflation	Important	Important (depends on negotiation)	Important	Somewhat important	Not important
Labor Cost	Not important	Not important	Very important	Not important	Somewhat important
Natural Resources	Not important	Important	Not important	Not important	Not important
Infrastructure Road and Port	Somewhat important	Important	Somewhat important	Not important	Not important
Infrastructure ITC	Somewhat important	Not important	Somewhat important	Not important	Somewhat important
Financial integration with home	Important	Not important	Not important	Important	Somewhat important

inflation, and exchange rate fluctuation (depicting exchange rate risk) are easily quantifiable and data exist for cross-country comparisons. However, other factors, such as work ethic and labor militancy, require expert judgment and rank the country based on best estimates (Cosset & Roy, 1991).

Therefore, it is important to weigh each of the variables to reflect their importance for the industry in which the firm operates. The weights are determined by surveying companies in specific industries. In the absence of the data, experts' views can be used for assigning weight to each factor. Some industries are consumer oriented and the firm's objective is to sell to the local market. In such case, purchasing power and economic growth are critical factors and will have a relatively higher weight than other factors. The retail industry, for example, looks for market growth and high purchasing power. Other firms select a country to reduce labor costs. The different weights can be estimated by sending a questionnaire to the industry expert. Weights must be normalized by dividing each weight by the total.

$$Wi = a_i / \Sigma a_i$$

where, a_i is the initial weight for factor i and Σa_i is the sum of all the weights and W_i is the normalized weight. Weights would be between 0 and 1; zero indicating that the factor is unimportant and 1 indicating that the factor is the only one impacting the decision. By applying the normalized weight to each factor for a country and adding them, we can identify the attractiveness of a country for a specific industry. By repeating the procedure for several different countries, we can obtain a ranking of the attractiveness of each country for an initial investment in a specific industry. Figure 7.1 shows the calculations for a specific location and an industry. It contains economic factors, political risk, labor, tax structure, capital resource availability, and general standard of living as in the case of an expatriate sent to the location. Column one shows the relative ranking of a country to the best performer. The second column is the weight depicting the importance for the industry. The third column is the normalized weight, and the forth column is the weighted importance (multiplication of column one by column three). The sum of the elements in column four provides the attractiveness of the location for a particular industry (Daniels, Radebaugh, & Sullivan, 2012).

The quantitative approach helps firms to allocate resources to the most attractive location. Recognizing that a firm has limited resources to internationalize, it must allocate its resources (both tangible and nontangible) to the location that provides the best result toward achieving its main objective. Even if the firm does not have limited resources, the above model

		Matrix for Country Selection			
		Relative Ranking (L:1-H:10)	Importance (L:0-H:1:0)	Weight*	Weighted Av. Country
Economic					
Rate of Eco. Growth		7	8	0.073	0.514
Price & Cost Stability		8	9	0.083	0.661
Exchange Rate Stability		8	9	0.083	0.661
Prvatization		7	6	0.055	0.385
Political Stability					
Political Process is Followed		9	5	0.046	0.413
Political Changes are Organized		8	6	0.055	0.440
Strong Legal System		6	6	0.055	0.330
Labor					
Low Militancy of Labor Force		4	8	0.073	0.294
Trained Labor		7	9	0.083	0.578
High Level Skills		7	2	0.018	0.128
Overall Labor Cost		6	10	0.092	0.550
Tax					
Preferential Tax Structure		5	8	0.073	0.367
					0.000
Capital Resources					0.000
Availability of Local Financing		8	2	0.018	0.147
Liquidity of Capital Market		7	2	0.018	0.128
General Living Environment					
Language		4	8	0.073	0.294
Similarity to Home Country		6	5	0.046	0.275
Cost of Living		7	6	0.055	0.385
			109	1.000	6.550
*Sum of the weights should add up to one (8/109=0.073).					

Figure 7.1 Country selection matrix.

helps any firm to screen out the locations that do not meet the minimum requirements of the firm. For instance, in the above example a location ranked at 6.55 would be selected if the firm's threshold level for investment is 6.0. However, if the threshold to invest is set at 7.0 or higher, the location would not be selected for investment. It is important to emphasize that the threshold level is set by each individual firm.

So far the discussion has focused on the location attractiveness and not on the firm's level of risk tolerance. It is possible to separate the risk element in the above model and provide a separate assessment of risk and attractiveness of a location. In other words, the risk tolerance of a firm is also an important parameter in the location selection process. It is obvious

Figure 7.2 Opportunity–risk matrix.

that firms should avoid countries where the risk is high and the opportunity for growth and profit are low. The most attractive conditions for a firm to establish operations are locations where there is high opportunity and low risk. However, locations that are risky can attract those firms that are risk takers, if the opportunities for growth and profitability are attractive. On the other hand, risk averse firms are attracted to low-risk, low-opportunity locations. The opportunity–risk matrix in Figure 7.2 demonstrates the four different possibilities.

We can define opportunity as the condition attractive for future business. This includes market growth, move toward an open economy, attempt to privatize state-owned enterprises, and trend toward political stability. It also implies economic and business openness and low degree of corruption.

Location Selection for a Firm Established in the Country

When a firm has operations in a foreign country, it becomes easier for it to evaluate its future strategy in that particular country. Among the issues to be considered by the headquarters is the desirability of further investment and resource allocation to the operation in that country. The two most important factors to be considered by the firm are the evaluation of attractiveness of the country and the competitiveness of the firm in that country. The firm's competitiveness can simply be defined by its market share. But it is possible to consider other factors besides market share. Other factors could include financial performance of the firm in that location, name recognition, and local know-how. The combination of country attractiveness and competitive position determines the most appropriate strategy choice for the firm. Depending upon those two factors, there are four different possibilities.

1. The first decision choice is for the situation in which the country is attractive and the company has a strong competitive position in the country. This is the most desirable situation and therefore it requires investment by firms in the location. Even if the resources generated within the country by investing firms are not enough for growing and building strategy, additional resources, including financial, should be brought in from the home country or even from a third country to make sure the operation remains competitive and that it continues its growth and success.

2. The other possibility is that the country is very attractive, but the firm's competitive position is not strong (see Figure 7.3). This could be due to a number of factors including lack of knowledge about the culture and other institutional factors. When such a weakness exists, it requires strengthening the position through a joint venture with a local firm that is familiar with the operation in the country and can help the firm to improve its situation there. In particular local firms can help with institutional factors, including government regulation, the competitive environment, and even with social and cultural factors. The firm must, however, be vigilant in the selection of a local partner. Many partnerships have failed because of a misunderstanding or cultural differences between the two firms.

3. In case a country is unattractive and the firm is not competitive in the country, the most advisable approach is to either harvest (slowly pull out of the country) or divest (to sell the operation to another firm).

4. Finally, if the firm's competitive situation is strong but the country is not attractive, then it requires a country specific strategy. This means

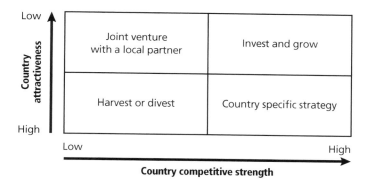

Figure 7.3 Country attractiveness/company strength matrix.

that the MNE must evaluate factors that make the overall environment unattractive and decide whether it makes sense for them to
keep operating or proceed to leave the location. For example, if the
unattractiveness is due to high risk, it is possible for the firm to find
ways to manage some of the risk and improve the overall condition.
The MNE can also use the location as a hub for a regional operation. In such a situation, it must do additional research and analysis
to make sure that it is not allocating resources to a losing cause.

Quantitative Indices for Countries

There are a number of institutions that build complex indices to rank various
countries from alternative perspectives of business attractiveness. Three of
these indices are listed below: Ease of doing business in a country, economic
freedom index, and the corruption perception index are discussed. It should
be noted that while each of this indices provide an insight to specific business
characteristics of the country, they are not without their critics.

Ease of Doing Business

The World Bank has developed an index for estimating the ease of doing
business in different countries (Table 7.2). This is an aggregate index that
includes the following factors: starting business, dealing with construction
permits, getting electricity, registering property, getting credit, protecting
minority business, paying taxes, trade across borders, enforcing contracts,
and resolving insolvency. Based on these factors the World Bank ranks
various countries. The top ranked country is Singapore, followed by New
Zealand, Hong Kong, Denmark, and Korea (South). The United States is
ranked number seven.

The index is structured in such a way that it compares each country
to the best practices, thus it is a relative measure. This is called distance to
frontier. The index has been criticized for not being grounded on strong
economic theory and being biased based on researchers' views. The World
Bank group itself has noted that it must be clear as to what the index measures specifically and what it does not.

Economic Freedom Index

The economic openness of a country is an important and attractive fea-
ture for foreign business operations. The less the government is involved

TABLE 7.2   Ease of Doing Business Rankings

Economy	Ease of Doing Business Rank	Starting a Business	Dealing with Construction Permits	Getting Electricity	Registering Property	Getting Credit	Protecting Minority Investors	Paying Taxes	Trading Across Border	Enforcing Contracts	Resolving Insolvency
Singapore	1	6	2	11	24	17	3	5	1	1	19
New Zealand	2	1	13	48	2	1	1	22	27	9	28
Hong Kong SAR, China	3	8	1	13	96	23	2	4	2	6	25
Denmark	4	25	5	14	8	23	17	12	7	34	9
Korea, Rep.	5	17	12	1	79	36	21	25	3	4	5
Norway	6	22	27	25	5	61	12	15	24	8	8
United States*	7	46	41	61	29	2	25	47	16	41	4
United Kingdom	8	45	17	70	68	17	4	16	15	36	13
Finland	9	27	33	33	38	36	76	21	14	17	1
Australia	10	7	19	55	53	4	71	39	49	12	14

*The rankings of economies with populations over 100 million are based on data for 2 cities.
Source: http://www.doingbusiness.org/rankings

in regulating the economic environment, the more attractive the location becomes for foreign investment and trade. There are a number of ways to assess the openness of the business environment. One index that provides a comparative ranking of various countries is the Economic Freedom Index.

The Economic Freedom Index (EFI)[1] is a composite index of 10 different economic factors that shows how open and free the economic and business possibilities are in each country. The index was created by The Heritage Foundation and *The Wall Street Journal* (see Table 7.3). According to The Heritage Foundation:

> Economic freedom is the fundamental right of every human to control his or her own labor and property. In an economically free society, individuals are free to work, produce, consume, and invest in any way they please, with that freedom both protected by the state and unconstrained by the state. In economically free societies, governments allow labor, capital and goods to move freely, and refrain from coercion or constraint of liberty beyond the extent necessary to protect and maintain liberty itself.[2]

The 10 factors included in the EFI are business freedom, trade freedom, monetary freedom, government size and spending, fiscal freedom, property rights, investment freedom, financial freedom, freedom from

TABLE 7.3 Economic Freedom Index Ranking

Rank	Country	Overall	Change
1	Hong Kong	89.7	0.0
2	Singapore	87.2	1.1
3	Australia	82.5	–0.1
4	New Zealand	82.3	0.2
5	Switzerland	81.9	0.8
6	Canada	80.8	0.4
7	Ireland	78.7	–2.6
8	Denmark	78.6	0.7
9	United States	77.8	–0.2
10	Bahrain	77.7	1.4

Source: http://www.heritage.org/index/

corruption, and labor freedom, which are each weighted equally. The top 10 countries, based on data for 2011, are listed below. An index value of 100 indicates a completely free country. The "change" column indicates the change from the previous year.

According to the Economic Freedom Index, Hong Kong is ranked number 1 in the world followed by Singapore and Australia. The United States is ranked 9th below Ireland and Denmark. Most of the developing countries, particularly the least developed ones, fall toward the bottom of the list. One could claim that the more open and free an economy is, the higher the rate of economic growth. However, this claim has been challenged by a number of scholars showing that there is no correlation between the index and economic growth and economic freedom (Sachs, 2006b). For example, BRIC countries that have shown a high rate of economic growth are ranked low in the index, with Brazil (113), Russia (143), India (124), and China (135).

From a foreign firm perspective, the more open the economy and the business environment, the more attractive the country is for foreign investment.

In other words, there is a positive relationship between economic freedom and foreign investment. At the same time, the more foreign investment and international activities, the greater would be the pressure to further open the economy and adjust the institution.

Corruption Perception Index

The Corruption Perception Index (CPI) is an index published by Transparency International that ranks various countries based on their degree of corruption in both the public and private sector. This is also an aggregated index that takes into account information from a number of different sources including regional development banks, the World Bank, the World Economic Forum, the Economic Intelligence Unit (EIU), Global Insight, and the IMD World Competitive Centre. The word *perception* is used since corruption is not transparent.

Perceptions are used because corruption—whether frequency or amount is to a great extent a hidden activity that is difficult to measure. Over time, perceptions have proved to be a reliable estimate of corruption. Measuring scandals, investigations or prosecutions, while offering "non-perception" data, reflect less on the prevalence of corruption in a country and more on other factors, such as freedom of the press or the efficiency of the judicial system. TI considers it of critical importance to measure both corruption and integrity, and to do so in the public and private sectors at global, national and local levels. The CPI is therefore one of many TI measurement tools that serve the fight against corruption.[3]

Based on the 2014 CPI ranking (Table 7.4), there are three countries that share the lowest corruption index: Denmark, New Zealand, and Singapore. The United States is ranked number 17. The most corrupt countries according to the CPI are Sudan, North Korea, and Somalia.

It is interesting to note that countries with the highest corruption perception index are the ones with either the lowest per capita income or are in a war situation. Thus, there seems to be a direct correlation between low income and a high degree of corruption. Nonetheless, what is not clear is

TABLE 7.4   Corruption Perception Index

Lowest Corruption		Highest Corruption	
1	Denmark	166	Eritrea
2	New Zealand	166	Libya
3	Finland	166	Uzbekistan
4	Sweden	169	Turkmenistan
5	Norway	170	Iraq
5	Switzerland	171	South Sudan
7	Singapore	172	Afghanistan
8	Netherlands	173	Sudan
9	Luxembourg	174	Korea (North)
10	Canada	174	Somalia

Source: http://www.transparency.org/policy_research/surveys_indices/cpi/2010/in_detail

the causality between these two factors. It is argued that a prerequisite for economic improvement is to address societal corruption. It is also possible to argue that to reduce corruption it is important to improve the economic situation of the country.

Clusters as Location

In selecting a foreign location, it is possible to look where clusters of similar companies are located. Joining clusters provides a number of benefits including the assurance and availability of supplies, availability of appropriate manpower, and adequate infrastructure. It also provides comfort to know that other firms have assessed the risk. Normally, governments offer a number of benefits to attract firms to a cluster.

Michael Porter popularized the concept of industrial cluster. Clusters are a geographic concentration of firms active in a related industry. Once established, clusters grow in two ways: new firms join already established ones in the cluster, or existing firms expand (Porter, 1998a). Dunning also argued that the pull of clustering and networking will have an increasing impact on the choice of location (Dunning, 2009).

The process of agglomeration continues over time leading to the expansion of the size of the cluster. In addition to the core expansion, the cluster expands through backward and forward linkages. The linkages create incentives for firms that supply to the cluster to physically establish themselves near their customers. Similarly, firms that use the products of a cluster are encouraged to establish themselves near their suppliers. Figure 7.4 shows the linkages

Clusters encourage both cooperation and competition. In many cases being in the geographic proximity of other firms doing similar types of activities provides an opportunity for collaborative work. Some of the advantages of being part of a cluster include the exchange of views on research

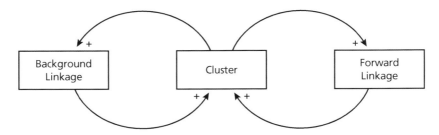

Figure 7.4 Backward and forward linkages.

and development, the ability to develop a working relationship with suppliers and buyers as a result of frequent visits and interaction, and the employee movement between the firms. All these factors are critical to improving the productivity of the cluster and contribute to its overall attractiveness.

However, clusters also face some drawbacks in terms of their competitiveness. Clearly competition will be very intense inside the cluster since all the members are competing for the same market segment. Additionally, because of the proximity of the competitors, the information flow is considerable within the cluster. Therefore firms normally lose their distinctive advantage. Information on technology, product design, pricing, and other competitive attributes of a firm are shared within the cluster in an informal way. Additionally, it is argued that a cluster eventually results in group thinking and does not lead to major innovation or new initiatives. Group thinking can also make the cluster rigid in the sense that all firms become comfortable doing what they are doing since others are doing the same thing, and therefore do not easily adapt to change.

Another disadvantage of clusters is that sometimes the main reason for establishing them disappears due to the success of the cluster itself. For example, if the reason for a U.S. software firm to go to Bangalore, India, was because of the relative lower labor costs, then the agglomeration of a software cluster in that region will lead to wage and cost increases resulting in losing the initial incentive for establishing the operation in that location. The demise of a cluster is the result of group thinking, losing the initial competitive advantage as a result of agglomeration, and the potential intense competition.

A number of emerging economies have attempted to develop their economy by promoting clusters around certain industries. As examples, India's famous effort to establish an IT cluster, the Persian Gulf countries established a petrochemical cluster (using cheap natural gas as feed stock), and Pakistan's textile cluster are just a few well-known clusters. Some of these clusters are built around cheap labor and others are built based on the availability and access of natural resources. However, creating technology-based clusters requires a special effort by the government, such as the establishment of a technology infrastructure as well as advanced and skilled labor. India has been quite successful in this regard. One way to promote the establishment and growth of clusters is to have outstanding universities to provide a stream of technical and entrepreneurial manpower. Porter observes that most advanced clusters are built around major universities.

Dynamics of Location Advantage Change

While moving overseas to a specific country provides a location advantage for a firm, this advantage could change over time. In other words, dynamic factors will change the advantages that a specific factor brings for the firm. For example, to lower labor costs, a firm may move to a specific country, but if many other firms follow the same strategy and invest in that particular country, the low-cost labor advantage may be temporary. The inflow of foreign investment over time will push labor costs higher and the competitive advantage gained from establishing operations in that location would disappear. In such a situation the firm may begin to seek to relocate to another country that still has a lower wage rate.

The firm may also want to re-evaluate the initial objective for going to the first country. Initially, the reason the firm established operations in the country was to capitalize on low labor costs. However, as the per capita income of the target country increases, the firm could also shift its strategy by focusing instead on the country as a potential market. That is, shift production to the second country to export to the first country.

This pattern has been observed in a number of Asian countries. Many firms initially moved to South Korea and Taiwan because of their low labor costs. But as these countries received a huge influx of foreign investment and their economy shifted from a low-income to a high-income country, they presented a potential market for multinationals. While many of those firms shifted production to China, they still operate in those countries but in a different capacity. Additionally, as these countries develop technological expertise, investment by multinationals has shifted from using a low-skilled workforce in those countries to establishing research and development activities and using a highly skilled workforce.

Notes

1. The Heritage Foundation formally names this index the Index of Economic Freedom.
1. http://www.heritage.org/research/features/index/chapters/pdf/index2008_execsum.pdf
2. http://www.transparency.org/policy_research/surveys_indices/cpi/2010/in_detail

8

The Internationalization Process of a Firm

This chapter describes the internationalization process as well as how value creation has been enhanced by internationalization. Different modes of entry and internationalization methods are also discussed. International business is essential in the economic activities of nations. It plays a critical role in the value creation of multinational enterprises. A significant portion of the revenues of multinationals is generated by their foreign activities. In many cases multinational foreign assets are also significant.

The increase in international business in the last decades can be attributed to many factors. Some of the factors that have contributed to the changes in the business landscape are the following:

■ The emergence of new technologies, as well as advances in the information and communications industries, have flattened the playing field especially for small and medium-size companies by providing them easier access to the global market.

Foundations of Global Business, pages 117–125
Copyright © 2016 by Information Age Publishing
All rights of reproduction in any form reserved.

- The continuous development of emerging markets such as China, India, Russia, Brazil, and other economies have created not only great opportunities for international business activities, but also potentially strong competitors.
- Multinational corporations from emerging economies have become global players and are competing with multinationals from developed countries.

Companies internationalize for different reasons. International business and commerce, for example, provide a great potential for value creation. Although there is no agreement on the definition of internationalization, there are several internationalization theories that try to explain why there are international activities. A group of internationalization theories can be classified as trade based theories. Among the trade theories, it is worth mentioning the following: absolute cost advantage (Adam Smith, 1776), comparative cost advantage (David Ricardo, 1817), gravity model of trade (Walter Isard, 1954), Heckscher-Ohlin model (Eli Heckscher, 1966 & Bertil Ohlin, 1952), Leontief paradox (Wassily Leontief, 1954), and market imperfection theory (Stephen Hymer, 1976, Charles P. Kindleberger, 1969, & Richard E. Caves, 1971).

In the next sections, we specifically explore some of the reasons for expanding.

Value Creation Through International Business

Profit maximization is one of the most important goals for every business. The bottom line can improve by either increasing revenues or by reducing costs. How internationalization can enhance a company's profit by increasing revenue and reducing cost is explained below.

Revenue Enhancing Through a Market Seeking Strategy

Firms can seek to increase profits through increasing sales. International expansion in search of new markets to increase profits is particularly important when demand in the company's home country (domestic market) is saturated or decreasing and demand exists abroad. Especially in small markets, the domestic market may be maturing so foreign markets, if they have a different life cycle than the home country, would provide revenue enhancing opportunities.

If we consider the scenario of a country where the domestic market for a certain product is saturated and a firm cannot further increase the demand for the product, in order to enhance revenue and maintain profits, the company would need to increase their sales volume. Since the domestic market has matured, an option to increase sales would be to seek foreign markets to increase the sales volume. Under these circumstances, one of the options firms have is to seek markets outside their domestic market. In other words, one of the revenue enhancing strategies is to expand internationally.

By determining the target sales, a company can estimate the level of demand that would be required to reach the domestic and foreign sales targets. In general, firms understand the domestic demand because they know the environment in which they operate. On the other hand, if international sales are successful, a firm may choose to focus on foreign sales to increase the foreign sales target in the future. The demand in an international market is much harder to forecast if they don't know the market. Thus, a firm may choose to focus more on clearly identified foreign sales. One way to do that is to internationalize by exporting to or investing in a new market. An increase in international activities will eventually increase foreign sales.

In general, firms invest in foreign markets to increase revenues. Such investments by firms in foreign markets may improve the economy of the host countries in the long run.

Cost Minimization Through a Resource-Seeking Strategy

Companies may also go abroad in order to gain access to resources that may not be readily available in the domestic market or may be costly in their home country. As domestic resources may be depleted and become more expensive, a firm might begin to look for foreign resources that are less costly.

The resources could be natural resources such as oil, copper, or water; man-made resources such as electricity; or human resources such as a talented, highly educated, or cheap workforce. China and India have been attracting a lot of foreign businesses due to their low-wage labor. China's widely available, low skilled, inexpensive labor force encourages producers to relocate there. India's highly educated, low-wage labor force draws companies who outsource customer service, software development, and other technical positions.

One of the cost reduction plans mentioned here is the resource-seeking strategy. With the resource-seeking strategy, the firm will get additional resources that are cheaper than the local ones from other countries. With the additional resources, the cost of the firm will be reduced. Firms invest in other countries to gain resources when the domestic ones are depleted or become expensive, and the problem is solved. However, we have seen that many firms need to withdraw the investment from one country and invest in another country because the resources in the host country become expensive as well. For example, the cost of the Chinese labor force was low a decade ago. However, the labor cost in China became much more expensive and many firms decided to shift their plants to other countries. It shows that the relationship we explained before is a short-term one. In the long run, we have a different relationship.

In the long run, the firm gets access to the resources from other countries, and the amount of the resources left in that country is reduced. When the resource is used, the resource availability will be lower and it will become scarce. Therefore, the cost of the resource will increase again and push the firm to go for another round of a resource-seeking strategy.

Competitive Positioning

Expanding operations in key places in order to gain a competitive advantage is another reason that companies choose to operate globally (Porter, 1990; Porter, 1998b). A company may expand an operation abroad in order to gain market share in that area or to prevent another company from gaining an advantage over them. They may need to follow their competitors into markets in order to prevent them from gaining an advantage. Or it is in its strategic domain to be the first company to enter the market in order to gain the first mover advantage. Firms invest in one country to gain a competitive position. Then the competitiveness will decrease when competitors try to match the strategy. In the end, firms need to invest in other countries to regain competitiveness again.

Following Customers or Suppliers

It may be in a company's best interest to remain in close proximity to their strategic customers or suppliers. If a supplier chooses to open a division in a foreign market, it may prove worthwhile for the customer to open an operation there as well and take advantage of the reduced transportation costs and potential new market for the end product. Another possibility is that the company may wish to follow the supplier to prevent one of its competitors from gaining an advantage by opening an operation close to the supplier's facility.

Avoiding Government Regulation

Many times companies chose a location in order to avoid government regulations that increase costs or make operating in a location more difficult, costly, and risky. For example, cruise lines register their ships in Panama in order to avoid taxes and stringent employment rules in the United States, even though the majority of passengers on the cruise ships are American citizens.

A company may choose to manufacture a product in a given country in order to avoid paying duties that would be imposed if the product was manufactured outside of the country and then imported into the country. The company may be trying to avoid lengthy procedures associated with opening a business in a foreign market. In China, for example, lengthy paperwork is required to be filled out in order to establish a wholly owned subsidiary. Multiple layers of government need to approve the application before the business can begin operations. The application and approval procedure can take years to finalize. Therefore a company may choose to form a joint venture or strategic alliance instead of a wholly owned subsidiary in order to avoid such a lengthy start-up time. Some countries enact legislation to protect their domestic companies. India and China, for example, prohibit foreign companies from having 100% ownership.

The discussion above highlights the primary factors that influence the internationalization of a firm. In the globalization era, firms internationalize in order to survive and to continue to grow.

Other Benefits to Internationalization

Risk diversification is another benefit of the internationalization of a firm. Risk diversification of investment has been studied from financial and strategic perspectives (Barney, 1997). Dependency on one location bears a location specific risk. Government regulations, economic downturn, and decline in demand are some of the examples of risk. Operating in different countries distributes the risk among various locations. It must also be noted that geographic diversification involves incremental risk. The countries to which a firm expands its operation to may have higher risk than the home country, thus increasing overall risk of the firm (Kwok & Reeb, 2000; Reeb, Kwok, & Baek, 1998).

Tax benefits are another advantage of an international business operation. Transfer pricing and cost have been noted as major advantages for firms operating internationally. Firms take advantage of tax rate differentials between various countries by allocating the cost to the country with a higher tax rate thus reducing the corporate taxable income as much as possible. This approach to value creation for stockholders has been questioned both legally and ethically. The Organisation for Economic Co-operation and Development (OECD) provided extensive rules for international business, particularly for transfer pricing (OECD, 2014).

The Process of Going International

Once a company decides to go abroad, there are different methods to internationalize. The method they choose can be based upon the level of experience they have in the host country, the amount of risk they are willing to undertake, and the amount of control they wish to keep. As companies gain more experience, they may change the method they use. Other well-known internationalization theories, which are now considered as traditional approaches, are Porter's Diamond model (1998), the eclectic paradigm theory by J. H. Dunning (1979, 1993, 2001), Vernon's product life cycle theory (1966), transaction cost theory (1988), the Uppsala model (1977), and the internationalization theory (Buckley & Casson, 1976; Coase, 1988; Dunning, 1976, 1979, 1993, 2001, 2009; Dunning, Van Hoesel, & Narula, 1997; Johanson & Vahlne, 1977; Porter, 1998b; Rugman, 1980; Rugman & Verbeke, 2004; Vernon, 1966).

A well-known model is the Uppsala model, which explains how firms gradually intensify their activities in foreign markets (Johanson & Vahlne, 1977). The key features of the model are the following: firms first gain experience from the domestic market before they move to foreign markets; then firms start their foreign operations from culturally and/or geographically close countries and move gradually to culturally and geographically more distant countries; finally, firms start their foreign operations by using traditional exports and gradually move to using more intensive and demanding operation modes, such as sales subsidiaries, both at the company and target country level. The Uppsala model also proposes that foreign sales begin with occasional export orders that are followed by regular exports. Finally, the firm will not commit higher levels of resources to the market until it has acquired increasing levels of experiential knowledge and therefore the internationalization evolves stepwise at a relatively *slow pace* because of local market regulations and/or organizational learning. As companies gain more experience, they can move through the various stages of internationalization. These are illustrated in Figure 8.1.

Figure 8.1 Internationalization stages.

This model has been challenged by Pan and Tse (2000). They argued that firms first decide whether to have a financial investment or not as part of their foreign strategy. If the decision is not to have a financial investment, then they use export/import, or strategic alliances as modes of entry. If the decision is to invest, then they chose either an international joint venture or a wholly owned subsidiary mode of entry (Pan & Tse, 2000).

Export–Import

This is the easiest way to expand internationally and globalize. Many companies start their international exposure through exporting their products or services and then move to other methods as their knowledge and comfort level increases.

Exporting requires a low level of investment, low risk, and also a lower return when compared to direct investment. The company retains operational control, but relinquishes the marketing and sales control to hosts. Resources are needed to address the increased activities necessary to support exporting. Management and staff may need to dedicate time to deal with a different language, different culture, and a different time zone. Financial personnel will need to process the different exchange rate transactions and implement various accounting changes.

Companies often underestimate the level of dedication that is needed to successfully export products. Many times, a company will choose a foreign agent or distributor that does not meet their expectations. Other common pitfalls include a failure to modify the product to meet the requirements of the foreign market, or not modifying the warranties or the instructions into the language of their new customers. Unfortunately, when the domestic market gets busy, serving the foreign market becomes a lower priority as people dedicate their time to serving the domestic customers. This reduces the sales and long-term profitability of the foreign market in the long run.

Companies import in order to lower the cost of a product, increase the quality of a product, or obtain a product that is not domestically available. This is easier than exporting and a customs broker can be of great assistance. They can fill out and file the required paperwork and categorize the product in such a way as to minimize the duty levied upon the goods. If needed, they can store the goods in bonded warehouses or foreign trade zones, or help process refunds for components that were assembled into products and then exported again.

Licensing

Licensing is an agreement between two companies where one company pays the other for the right to use their intangible asset, such as a patent, copyrights, technical knowledge, or specialized processes.

For example, General Electric chose to license Asian suppliers to manufacture certain grades of copper clad laminates when the product became a commodity. It did not make sense for this product to be manufactured in the United States. Cheaper labor and good access to natural resources enabled this product to be manufactured in Asia, then imported and sold in the United States in a market where they would not be able to compete had this agreement not been in place.

Franchising

Franchising is a form of licensing in which one company allows the other company to use their trademark and also assists them in the operation of the business. This method is common in the fast-food industry. Franchising takes advantage of well-known company logos allowing products to be introduced into areas where the product would not have been popular if the name didn't have a high level of recognition. It also keeps the product consistent.

For example, since their inception in 1974 Subway restaurants have focused on franchising and have experienced phenomenal growth. They are aiming to become the number one *quick service restaurant* chain in the world. There are more than 37,000 Subway® locations throughout the world. In recent years, about 70% of the new franchises have been purchased by existing owners. The investment capital required to open a franchise is anywhere between $84,300 and $258,300 (Subway.com, 2014).

Outsourcing and Strategic Alliances

Outsourcing is the practice of contracting for the manufacture of goods or services outside of the home country. This arrangement works best when transportation costs and inventory management are not major factors. The goods may need to travel in bulk back to the home country, then be separated and repackaged into smaller orders before shipment to the customer. With production in a foreign facility, product in transit, and stock in the home country, inventory management can be complicated and cost prohibitive to accurately track in detail.

Drawbacks of this method include the loss of operational control, cultural barriers, costs, and dependence on another company. A strategic alliance is an agreement between two or more companies to cooperate in business, enabling the business to take place. Without this cooperation the business would not be possible. This arrangement helps companies to spread or reduce costs, gain access to needed resources, sidestep government regulations, and minimize political and economic risk. It allows a company to concentrate on their core competencies while addressing competitive concerns.

Joint Venture

A joint venture is a business arrangement in which two or more companies share ownership of another company. The more companies that are involved, the less control each has over the newly formed company. About 50% of joint ventures fail for various reasons. Partners may have different objectives for the joint venture, a different sense of priority of the joint venture, or disagreements over control may occur. Other sources of friction include cultural clashes or resentment arising when one company thinks it is unfairly doing the majority of the work while the other partners are not as dedicated.

Wholly Owned Subsidiary

A foreign company that is separate from but fully owned by the parent company is a wholly owned subsidiary. This structure allows the company to retain the most control, but it is also the most risky method. It is generally chosen by large companies with experience in international business and available resources that can be dedicated to the start-up and ongoing operation of the subsidiary. It is much more labor intensive than the other internationalization methods mentioned previously.

9

Cross-Cultural Management

In this chapter we will define culture and its key components, and present fundamental issues of successfully managing cross-culturally with a global mindset. We will explain why we should appreciate cultural differences and make it an asset to become successful in global operations. We will provide an explanation on how a global manager can be interculturally effective in managing change in global organizations.

Globalization has been the most important phenomenon that has challenged the mindset, decision making, and strategic direction of most companies' leadership. Globalization has been defined in a variety of ways throughout the last century with one common trend among the definitions: interdependency. *The New York Times* columnist Thomas Friedman defines globalization in his book *The Lexus and the Olive Tree* as "the inexorable integration of markets, capitals, nation-states, and technologies in ways that allow individuals, groups, corporations, and countries to reach around the world farther, faster, deeper, and cheaper than ever before." (Friedman, 2000) What this definition implies is that managers need not just address

Foundations of Global Business, pages 127–139
Copyright © 2016 by Information Age Publishing
All rights of reproduction in any form reserved.

globalization in every managerial decision, but also see the opportunities that arise with it.

The biggest challenge that a manager is facing in the era of globalization is adapting to cultural differences and the ability to make appropriate decisions. A manager with a global mindset and knowledge about cultural issues should be able to make efficient, appropriate, and ethical decisions given the opportunities and constraints. For examples, the current CEO of PepsiCo, Indra Nooyi, and the Coca-Cola CEO Muhtar Kent represent leaders with the global mindset and cross-cultural awareness due to their decisions and background. Both CEOs have had significant cross-cultural interaction and exposure through background and international assignments around the world. Therefore, because of their cultural background, exposures, and experiences, they have a good global mindset.

The management style that matches the international business environment will reduce the cost of doing business internationally. With a lower cost of doing international business, firms will expand their operations internationally. When international business becomes more important for the firms, the management style needs to be adjusted to better suit international business.

Global managers need to have a mindset that enables them to clearly link end users' interests with the company's strategic goals and objectives. This means a manager has to engage cross-cultural employees in the success of the company skillfully and ethically in addition to efficiently building an organizational structure that is capable of delivering the best output possible.

Lane et al. articulated that global managers need to have the capability to skillfully and effectively deal with the following four factors so they can execute a plan with some degree of predictability (Lane, Maznevski, Dietz, & DiStefano, 2009).

- Interdependency: The globalized world has led companies, governments, and citizens of the world in becoming interdependent.
- Variety: CEOs have to deal with a variety of issues, internally and externally (nationally and internationally) and therefore, having diverse educational and experiential background is very useful.
- Ambiguity: Because so many factors are at play in operating in the global economy, it will create a high degree of ambiguity. Thus, leadership shall have the ability to identify essential factors that require focus and attention.
- Fast flux: So many things (i.e., public policies, market conditions, competitors, labor market, etc.) are moving so rapidly with the

fast pace (24/7) that requires CEOs to make decisions in these circumstances.

The above factors highlight some of the key issues that a global manager has to deal with systemically across different time zones and cultures. This demands a prudent application of human resource management because so many factors—horizontal, vertical, and over time—are at play. Additionally, so many exogenous and endogenous variables may shock an organization. Successful leaders are capable of applying this system when formulating their strategic direction and in their daily activities. For example, Samuel J. Palmisano, IBM's CEO, was capable of articulating clearly the goals and objectives of the company and adding values to them (Hempel, 2011). The same is true for Zhang Ruimin, the CEO of Haier. The company was operating in China, but the CEO was applying American innovation, Japanese quality control methods, and Chinese collectivist culture (Haier.com, 2014).

However, in the long run, these four factors will also be shifted. As we discussed earlier, the interdependency creates a cultural convergence that to some degree reduces the variety and ambiguity. When variety and ambiguity are reduced, managing international businesses may become easier, which in turn facilitates a higher degree of success.

One consequence of increasing globalization is the high degree of interdependence and interconnectedness among the different parties in business relationships. The idea that most organizations have significant independence from micro and macro perspectives in their decision making is long gone. Generally organizations have a higher degree of independence at the micro level than the macro because micro issues are internal factors of production, such as human resources. The macro variables are exogenous (domestic or international) and could impact organizations unexpectedly. Interdependence refers to the extent at which organizations, communities, countries, or people depend on each other in the production process. Barry Jones explains that organizations may not foresee themselves as a worldwide community. He argues that organizations need to consider every possible impact that their decisions may have on other organizations and related entities (i.e., customers, suppliers, etc.) around the world (Jones, 1995).

In many aspects global managers are facing an imperfect world of cultural differences that bring in significant opportunities and hindrances. Organizations and their leaders need to carefully navigate in this muddy river to be able to survive. One of the most difficult aspects of managing globally is being able to deal with cross-cultural issues ethically. Organizations frequently encounter ethical dilemmas that raise organization-wide questions regarding their stance on corruption, briberies, slavery, underage employment, racial and gender discrimination, human rights issues, and other aspects that could dramatically change. In the book, *Management Across Cultures*, Steers et al. note that organizations can approach this issue in two polarized ways (Steers, Sanchez-Runde, & Nardon, 2010). First, a global organization needs a clear ethical compass to guide their organizational actions. This approach tries to standardize ethical behaviors throughout all the different environments where the organization is operating.

The second approach that is used in some organizations is to not judge what is right or wrong. These organizations believe that right or wrong only exists in the eye of the beholder (Steers, Sanchez-Runde, & Nardon, 2010). Both views approach the issue of ethical values in different cultures somewhat differently. However, organizations need to have clear and transparent ethical guidelines and implementation policies. Otherwise, problems can arise from incongruence among decisions within the organization.

Culture and Global Management

The same is true for Mr. Zhang, the CEO of Haier. In order for organizations to be successful in the global economy, they should consider all cultural aspects that could directly and indirectly affect their outcomes in terms of their global strategy, business relationships, employees' performance, and daily operations. Leadership's ability to adapt to the different environments and expectations that cross-cultural management requires starts with correctly identifying the mix of cultures involved in business partnerships.

Defining Culture

To fully understand the impact that culture has on organizational behavior, managers need to clearly define culture and its impact on the organization. Throughout the last century several definitions have evolved universally to comprehend what culture entails. Sir Edward B. Taylor warned about the complexity of defining culture due to the comprehensive characteristics that need to be included if the term is used to generalize groups of people. Anthropologist Alfred Kroeber defines culture "as a set of shared attitudes, values, goals, and practices that characterizes an institution, organization or group" (Kluckhohn & Strodtbeck, 1961).

UNESCO recognizes culture in its Universal Declaration on Cultural Diversity as "the set of distinctive spiritual, material, intellectual and emotional features of society or a social group, and that it encompasses, in addition to art and literature, lifestyles, ways of living together, value systems, traditions and belief" (UNESCO, 2002). Other authors have recognized culture as a synonym for civilization, defining the overall characteristics that identify a group of people or community as local culture. For Ruth Benedict, a sociologist, "culture, like an individual, is a more or less consistent pattern of thought and action" (Benedict, 1989). Anthropologist Clifford Geertz sees culture as "the means by which people communicate, perpetuate and develop their knowledge about attitudes towards life" (Geertz, 1973). If behaviors can be understood and predicted, managers are able to direct multicultural organizations better to their goal. Kluckhohn and Strodtbeck define culture as a shared, commonly held body of beliefs and values that define the "shoulds" and "oughts" of life (Kluckhohn & Strodtbeck, 1961). Culture is not a combination of the properties of the "average citizen" of a country. Hofstede defines it as "the collective programming of the mind which distinguishes one group or category from another" (Hofstede, 1984).

Steers et al. explained the need that managers have to understand normative behaviors derived from organizational cultures to be able to successfully guide organizations. Although all of the definitions above are a bit different, they group a thought that implies that culture might be static and shared among everybody in an organization, region, and country and ignore capability for evolution within the culture. As we saw in the previous chapter, globalization has created an environment for those citizens who are linked together to evolve toward one culture. Culture can also be seen as the cultivation of progressive refinement of human behavior or the study of perfection.

Since culture can evolve faster than physical or biological aspects in humans, culture becomes the method used to survive and evolve as a community or civilization. Organizations have to be able to handle the adaptation that individuals go through on a daily basis in their ever-changing environment, without affecting those aspects that make the local and organizational culture unique.

Components of Culture

Assessing cultural impact is the first step for organizations to examine when managing in a cross-cultural environment. The second step is to understand the different levels or components that conform to what is known as someone's culture. Culture is shared, learned, and organized among a group, region, or country. The word "shared" means that it has to be acknowledged as common by more than one person. Culture is "learned" because it is transmitted through the process of learning and interacting with the surrounding environment. Culture is "organized" (or systematic) because culture is not a random assortment of elements, but a well-organized system of values, attitudes, beliefs, and behavioral meanings related to each other. Individual behavior can be divided into different levels that assess the influence that different aspects including culture have on individuals. Hofstede presented in his 1980 dimensions of culture assessment three different levels of mental programming that explained how individuals behave in regular circumstances (Thomas & Peterson, 2014).

Hofstede called the first level universal or biological. This level comprises all of human nature expected behavior such as eating when hungry or sleeping when tired. He suggested all individuals and human beings share this level of attributes across cultures since birth. The second level of culture refers to those behaviors that are learned and specific to a particular group of individuals. Most definitions of culture describe the characteristics found in this level since they can be easier to identify as a group. Hofstede names this level "culture" in an attempt to clarify what most people named culture in human behavior. The third level of individual behavior reflects the characteristics that are specific to the individual and are not shared among a group of people. Hofstede named this level "personality" and it is a product of inherited and learned behavior.

The importance of identifying the different levels of individual behavior for managers is that confusing one group with another can lead to the misinterpretation of a culture and will impact organizational performance. Managers must be able to differentiate the types of behavior and their roots before generalizing anything as cultural behavior.

For example, if a firm's home country has a low power distance where high level managers and middle level managers interact easily, but a high power distance characterizes the host country's culture, then there is a strong possibility of a culture clash between the business's parent company and the subsidiary. However, through the interaction between the headquarters and the subsidiary, there will be a convergence of cultures that creates a new "business culture" unique to the firm's headquarters and its subsidiary, otherwise the venture will be likely to fail. The extent to which the headquarters and the subsidiary create a business culture depends on the size of the firm and the size of the subsidiary. In many cases, large multinationals operating in a small country have a significant impact on the culture of their host country. For example, a U.S. MNC that is operating in Brazil has to modify its operation there because of the collectivist cultural behavior.

Geert Hofstede has done a major groundbreaking study of national and organizational cultures. His research on corporate cultures defined six dimensions that shape the organizational culture of a company:

Individualism versus collectivism: This dimension refers to how employees interact with each other. In an individualist scenario, employees tend to work individually and the interaction with others is minimal; while in a collectivist scenario, teamwork is the norm and is promoted by the company.

Power distance: This dimension alludes to the hierarchical relationships between subordinates and leaders. The Power Distance Index can be viewed as an organizational leadership style that varies from autocratic to participative. effectively, Low Power Distance organizations are characterized by leadership styles that empower subordinates and treat them in a very proximate way. High Power Distance organizations have cultures where the leadership styles are more authoritarian, with less regard for any initiatives from subordinates.

Uncertainty avoidance: This refers to how much members of a society are anxious about the unknown, and as a consequence attempt to cope with anxiety by minimizing uncertainty. In cultures with strong uncertainty avoidance, people prefer explicit rules (e.g., about religion and food) and formally structured activities, and employees tend to remain longer with their present employer. In cultures with weak uncertainty avoidance, people prefer implicit or flexible rules or guidelines and informal activities. Employees tend to change employers more frequently.

Masculinity and femininity: This refers to the value placed on traditional male or female roles (as understood in most Western cultures). In so-called "masculine" cultures, people (whether male or female) value competitiveness, assertiveness, ambition, and the accumulation of wealth and material possessions. In so-called "feminine" cultures, people value relationships and quality of life.

Long versus short-term orientation: This deals with a society's "time horizon" or the importance attached to the future versus the past and present. In long-term oriented societies, people value actions and attitudes that affect the future: persistence/perseverance, thrift, and shame. In short-term oriented societies, people value actions and attitudes that are affected by the past or the present, such as protecting one's own face, respect for tradition, and reciprocation of greetings, favors, and gifts.

Indulgence versus restraint: This refers to how much a society allows relatively free gratification of basic and natural human desires related to enjoying life and having fun. Restraint stands for a society that suppresses gratification of those needs and regulates it using social norms.

Global Mindset and Managerial Skills

Managers in multinational organizations face different challenges than traditional managers. Before identifying some of these challenges, it is important to evaluate the managerial styles and skillsets that managers in multinational organizations must have to overcome cross-cultural challenges. Managers' skillsets can be classified differently according to their degree of exposure to different cultures. It is difficult to encounter managers that do not find themselves impacted in the era of globalization, even though their organizations have been operating locally and are technically "domestic" companies. Global managers refers to individuals engaged in cross-cultural management who have a global mindset and are capable of interpreting situations, conflicts, opportunities, and weaknesses from all angles. Managers must identify their limitations regarding cross-cultural challenges and try to address them beforehand to prevent conflicts within the organization and among partners.

Lane et al. have discussed the building blocks of global competency in a stepwise format. While we do use their concepts as a base, we think it is a 360-degree format and concept (see Figure 9.1). This global competency is composed of a foundation of global knowledge and four levels of traits, attitudes, and orientations. Individuals with open-minded characteristics and the ability to learn would be able to manage effectively in the global

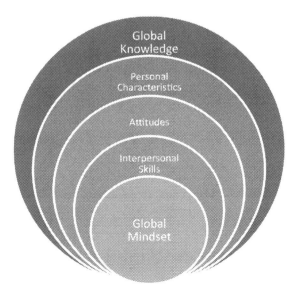

Figure 9.1 Global competencies.

setting. A global leader should be nearly perfect in terms of the stated characteristics or be capable of acquiring advice from councils with expertise (Lane et al., 2009).

Personal Integrity and Global Mindset

What is personal integrity? How do we acquire personal integrity? Do we acquire it genetically? What are the roles that family, schooling, and societies as a whole play in instilling ethical behavior in each individual? All of the mentioned factors influence personal integrity and have many implications for individuals, organizations, and society. It is not easy to quantify the influence of these factors on integrity or to quantify integrity itself. In the era of globalization, personal integrity has a significant influence on acquiring a global mindset. Lane et al. define a global mindset as "the capacity to develop and interpret criteria for personal and business performance, that are independent from the assumptions of a single context; and to interpret those criteria appropriately in different contexts" (Lane et al., 2009, 2).

In the current worldwide economic situation, being culturally aware and interculturally competent is a must for success in this highly competitive international market. Successful businesses from all over the world are competing for the top spots in international industries. Being business savvy and having a good track record at home is no longer enough to secure the best roles in the global aspect. A global mindset is what organizations need to be successful in a global role. They need to be capable of adjusting to different environments and have the ability to work effectively with other international businesses. Scholars have identified two constructs that comprise a global mindset: cognitive complexity and cosmopolitanism. To have a global mindset, an individual or an organization must have the ability to perceive multiple aspects of complex issues from multiple perspectives (cognitive complexity), while also having an openness to different cultural experiences and a willingness to explore, learn, and change (cosmopolitanism).

In addition to these competencies, there are four types of knowledge in which global mindsets operate. To achieve a good global mindset is to develop self-awareness, awareness of others, the relationship between cultures, and the characteristics of the self and others. The four types of knowledge an organization should have to operate their global mindset are knowledge about self (CEO), knowledge about others (other CEOs), knowledge about their own organization, and knowledge about other organizations.

The value of a global mindset lies in enabling the company to combine speed with accurate response. The benefit of a global mindset derives from the fact that, while the company has a grasp of the needs of the local market, it is also able to build cognitive bridges across these needs, as well as between these needs and the company's own global experience or capabilities. The key word of global mindset is cultivation, and the shape of that mindset is our interpretation of the world around us.

How does an individual or organization cultivate self-consciousness regarding their current market? The first approach is to ask managers or organizations to articulate their beliefs about the subject area. The second approach is to conduct a comparative analysis of how different people or companies appear to interpret the same reality. On the other hand, companies can cultivate exposure to and increase knowledge of diverse cultures and markets in two ways. First, facilitate such knowledge building at the level of individuals. Second, companies should build diversity in the composition of the people making up the company. This could provide companies with lots of cultural background and ideas.

Both approaches are essential for every company and complement each other. The first focuses on building cognitive diversity inside the mindsets of individuals (top executives and workers), and the second focuses on assembling a diverse knowledge base across the organization's members.

Challenges of Operating Globally

When organizations engage in international business, it is certain that they will face the additional challenge of cultural differences. Identifying the types of issues or challenges organizations face demands that managers prepare themselves in advance of assignments to be able to avoid conflicts. Scholars highlight that a majority of the challenges that will arise are interpersonal communication and performance rather than technical and organizational behavior. The fact is that people's cultures form organizational identities. Some of the most important challenges explained below were identified from Steers et al. (2010):

a. **Develop a learning strategy for professional development.** Managers need to develop a strategy for professional development that would guide them throughout their career. When managers face cultural differences in their environments, it is important that managers have a strategy in the short run of how to resolve and act through adversity, as part of a long-term goal.

b. **Basic knowledge of different cultures.** The differences between cultures cannot only bring up conflicts or challenges, but also opportunities and advantages for businesses to be successful. Managers in cross-cultural organizations need to understand which ones are the main differences between the cultures in a new working environment to fully address the needs of all parties involved in the organization. This includes a self-assessment of the manager's own culture that will allow him or her to find the most important similarities and possible conflict issues.

c. **Action strategies.** Successful managers are able to deal with people of different cultures, which will be helpful in minimizing conflicts and maximizing results and efficiency. Understanding how people in other cultures might react to different circumstances can be extremely helpful to managers. Managers need to know how and when to act to create an environment that would foster success and not raise conflict. It is the manager's responsibility to know in advance how the differences in cultures will affect interactions and communication among the key stakeholders. An absence of a plan on how to mitigate the cultural shock can create organizational conflicts that will negatively impact overall performance. On the other hand, if a manager develops plans of action according to the environment, it will be easier to identify the right moments for intervention, which will most likely reduce cultural barriers.

d. **Ethical and legal differences.** As noted before, knowing the differences in ethical values between cultures should minimize the cultural shock experienced by managers. It is important for managers to know what is ethical and legal in the place of work in order to take actions accordingly. Multinational organizations can face difficult challenges when two countries that they have operations in have different ethical values. Adapting and trying to respond legally and ethically would be the right approach. Adhering to the legal system of each country is one of the first steps in entering into that country's market. Of course, there are many gray areas between what is legal and ethical in each culture. If a manager is not careful in dealing with these issues appropriately, it can become costly for the organization and the individual. Overall, the organizations must assess these differences, and managers must become protectors of an ethical identity throughout the organization.

e. **Leadership roles vary between cultures.** Managing organizations and leading organizations means different things in different cultures. The expectations of a leader can drastically change depending on the place where the organization is operating. Managers need to understand the employees' expectations and try to meet that outlook in order to gain respect and avoid misunderstandings in the long run. Successful managers are capable of turning the challenges to opportunities for the organization and themselves. Also, managers who have the capacity to use diversity in a cross-cultural setting are able to add value to the organization.

Managing Change in Global Organizations

Change in organizations is a continuous process because in the global arena, changes are taking place at the macro level, industry level, labor market, and also in consumer preferences. Therefore, an organization has to respond to any or all of the mentioned factors to stay in business. However, the word "change" has a broad definition in regards to an organization. We can articulate three scenarios; crisis change, reactive change, and anticipatory change. First, some companies (i.e., GM, Ford, and Chrysler) had to make drastic changes in 2009 in their strategy in order to survive because they were not prepared for unanticipated macroeconomic shocks in the marketplace and changes in consumers' preferences in the global economy. We can define these scenarios as "crisis change." In these cases, organizations' survivability are at stake and significant changes in organization are demanded.

There are other cases (i.e., Toyota in 2010) in which companies react to the consumers complaints due to quality control and other changes in the market conditions. We define these circumstances as "reactive change." These cases are not as severe as the first cases but require the serious and timely attention of the organization. For example, Toyota responded aggressively to the recall and offered 24/7 services to its customers. If an organization does not respond to the new condition by making appropriate changes, then the situation can become too costly for the organization in terms of the bottom line, market share, and reputation. The third case is defined as "anticipatory change" in which market circumstance and firm strategy are important. For example, the demographic changes within the United States and internationally are demanding that institutions of higher education carefully assess their recruitment strategy. In these cases organizations are proactive in assessing their status in the marketplace, and have formulated appropriate responses.

Evaluation of globalization has forced organizations to be on standby in addressing any one of the noted changes. Many organizations have a review process every 3 to 5 years to ensure the growth of their business. Perhaps, they need a division called "change," with the responsibility of reviewing their strategy. Those organizations that are on continuous stand-by might be more prepared to avoid big shocks and try to ensure the growth of their business. For example, Kodak, a well-known global company, was forced into bankruptcy in January 2012. This is an example of a pioneering 19th century company that did not appropriately analyze the changing marketplace and consumer demand.

Conclusions

This chapter highlights key issues that global managers have to be knowledgeable about to be successful in leading their organization. The CEOs of three companies (PepsiCo, IBM, and Haier) discussed in this chapter have been very successful in functioning effectively in the global marketplace. The economic environment has become increasingly global and thus cultures are converging for certain segments of society. An interesting aspect of this trend is that increasingly companies are hiring international CEOs. Organizations are now focusing on the qualities and skills of the workers instead of purely focusing on their nationalities. It is a challenge for a company to expand to another country while still keeping its original brand because they want to cater to other countries as well. Companies must adapt to the culture of the country they want to enter or expand to while maintaining some authenticity. Experience has shown that global companies gain advantages by adapting to the specific cultures they choose to operate in. Therefore, they should research the cultural norms, attitudes, and behaviors, so that they are less likely to experience a "cultural shock" and can fit into the new culture without much difficulty. This will help global companies satisfy their customers' needs, which will eventually lead to the company being more profitable.

10

Corporate Social Responsibility and Environmental Sustainability

The aim of this chapter is to explain concepts of corporate social responsibility (CSR) and sustainable development in accordance with environmental sustainability. Also, we present the advantages and disadvantages of CSR and examine the latest debates and discussion on these subjects. Additionally, we will discuss the Global Reporting Initiative (GRI) framework concepts and the impact of sustainability and corporate social responsibility on businesses performance.

Corporate Social Responsibility

Corporate social responsibility or CSR is broadly defined as the "economic, legal, ethical, and discretionary expectations that society has of organizations at a given point in time" (Buchholtz & Carroll, 2012). Through the concept of CRS, businesses and organizations are given moral, ethical, and

Foundations of Global Business, pages 141–158
Copyright © 2016 by Information Age Publishing
All rights of reproduction in any form reserved.

philanthropic responsibilities in addition to the traditional responsibilities of earning a fair return for investors and complying with the required laws.

In other words, the traditional view that suggests that the primary and sole responsibility of a corporation is to its owners has been broadened. Corporate social responsibility demands organizations be responsible for other constituencies such as employees, suppliers, customers, the local community, local, state, and federal governments, environmental groups, and other special interest groups, in addition to their shareholders. The various groups affected by the actions of an organization are usually called stakeholders.

The concept of corporate social responsibility refers to initiatives to assess and take responsibility for a company's effects on the environment and impact on social welfare. CSR focuses on how an organization encompasses social and ethical responsibility when determining how to secure profits. The United Nations has stated that the concept of CSR is directly interchangeable with an organization's corporate responsibility for citizenship, social enterprise, sustainability, and corporate ethics. Other philosophers have stated that CSR refers to a voluntary code of ethics that multinational organizations could implement (Adams, Tashchian, & Shore, 2001). MNCs today realize that in order to operate ethically and within the confines of corporate social responsibility, organizations need to rely on integrated relationships with stakeholders in hopes of developing long term value.

Freeman (1984) states that stakeholders are "any group or individual who can affect or is affected by the achievement of the firm's objectives." The stakeholder theory is directly related to Freeman's statement as it describes the need for MNCs to focus on incorporating internal and external stakeholders into their business decisions. The stakeholder theory discusses that a MNC's internal stakeholders (owners, customers, and suppliers) and external stakeholders (the government, environment, and local communities) are vital to the success of any organization. When a MNC views its stakeholders as an integrated member of their business, this facilitates an easier development and adaption to sustainability and CSR initiatives across all business functions and departments. The effects of increased sustainability through integrated stakeholder partnerships can lead to increases in financial performances as well as greater brand image recognition (Asgary & Li, forthcoming 2015; Freeman, 2010; Porter and Kramer, 2006).

Some scholars (Adams et al., 2001; Asgary & Mitschow, 2002; Sethi, 2005) have discussed voluntary codes of ethics and proposed new codes for multinational corporations. Laplume et al. (2008), Lopez-De-Pedro and Rimbau-Gilabert, (2012) conducted a comprehensive survey of stakeholder theory and proposed new criteria to expand the stakeholder model (Laplume, Sonpar, & Litz, 2008; Lopez-De-Pedro & Rimbau-Gilabert, 2012).

Although CSR is related to business ethics, the concept is different. While CSR encompasses the economic, legal, ethical, and discretionary responsibilities of organizations, business ethics usually focuses on the moral judgments and behavior of individuals and groups within organizations. Thus, the study of business ethics may be regarded as a component of the larger study of corporate social responsibility (Buchholtz & Carroll, 2012).

The economic responsibility of business corporations is to produce goods and services efficiently, profitably, and to keep shareholder interests. On the other hand, society's expectation is that business corporations will produce goods and services that are needed and desired by customers and sell those goods and services at a reasonable price. Regarding the legal responsibilities of a business corporation, it is expected that a business will comply with the established laws. The ethical responsibilities of a business corporation include societal expectations that go beyond the law. Thus it is expected that business corporations will conduct their affairs in a fair and just way. In other words, business corporations need to be proactive to anticipate and meet the norms of society even if those norms are not formally enacted into law. Finally, one of the discretionary responsibilities of a business corporation is to behave as good citizens. Thus, business corporations are expected to behave as good citizens and be involved in philanthropic support of programs benefiting a community or the nation, which may also involve donating employee expertise and time to worthy causes.

The nature and scope of corporate social responsibility has changed over the years. The concept of CSR has been in wide use since the 1960s. But, while the economic, legal, ethical, and discretionary expectations placed on business corporations may differ, it is probably accurate to say that all societies at all points in time have had some degree of expectation that business corporations would act responsibly, by some definition.

Around the beginning of the 20th century, a backlash against large corporations began to gain momentum. Big business was criticized for being too powerful and for practicing antisocial and anticompetitive practices. Laws and regulations, such as the Sherman Antitrust Act, were enacted to rein in large corporations and to protect employees, consumers, and society at large. The labor movement also called for greater social responsiveness on the part of business. Between 1900 and 1960 the business world gradually began to accept additional responsibilities other than making a profit and obeying the law.

In the 1960s and 1970s, the Civil Rights Movement, consumerism, and environmentalism affected society's expectations of business. Based on the general idea that those with great power have great responsibility, many called for the business world to be more proactive in ceasing to cause societal problems and starting to participate in solving societal problems. Some legal mandates were placed on businesses that related to equal employment opportunity, product safety, worker safety, and the environment. Furthermore, society began to expect businesses to voluntarily participate in solving societal problems whether they had caused the problems or not. This was based on the view that corporations should go beyond their economic and legal responsibilities and accept responsibilities related to the advancement of society. This view of corporate social responsibility is the prevailing view in much of the world today.

Arguments For and Against Corporate Social Responsibility

The major arguments for and against corporate social responsibility are shown in Table 10.1. The economic argument against CSR is closely associated with the American economist Milton Friedman, who argued that the primary responsibility of business is to make a profit for its owners, while complying with the law. According to this view, the self-interested actions of

TABLE 10.1 Arguments For and Against Corporate Social Responsibility

	For	Against
Utilitarian Argument	Corporation created and continued to create many social problems. Therefore, the corporate world should assume responsibility for addressing these problems.	Taking on social and moral issues is not economically feasible. Corporations should focus on earning a profit for their shareholders and leave social issues to others.
Competitive Argument	In the long run, it is in the corporations' best interest to assume social responsibilities to ensure future success and potentially avoid governmental regulation.	Social responsibility creates additional costs placing corporations at a competitive disadvantage relative to corporations that are not socially responsible.
Capability Argument	Large corporations have huge reserves of human and financial capital. They should devote at least some of their resources to addressing social issues.	Those who are most capable should address social issues. Those in the corporate world are not equipped to deal with social problems.

millions of participants in free markets will, from a utilitarian perspective, lead to positive outcomes for society. If the operation of the free market cannot solve a social problem, it becomes the responsibility of the government, not the business, to address the issue.

The competitive argument recognizes the fact that addressing social issues creates additional cost to a business that in turn will hurt the competitive position of the business relative to other businesses. This argument is particularly relevant in a globally competitive environment if businesses in one country expend assets to address social issues, but those in another country do not. According to Buchholtz and Carroll (2012), since CSR is increasingly becoming a global concern, the differences in societal expectations around the world can be expected to lessen in the coming years. The effects of increased sustainability through integrated stakeholder partnerships can lead to increases in financial performances as well as greater brand image recognition and competitive advantages (Asgary & Li, forthcoming 2015).

Finally, some argue that businesses are ill equipped to address social problems. This capability argument suggests that business executives and managers are typically well trained in the ways of finance, marketing, and operations management, but not well versed in dealing with complex societal problems. Thus, they do not have the knowledge or skills needed to deal with social issues. This view suggests that corporate involvement in social issues may actually make the situation worse. Part of the capability argument also suggests that corporations can best serve societal interests by sticking to what they do best, which is providing quality goods and services and selling them at an affordable price to people who desire them.

There are several arguments in favor of corporate social responsibility. One view, held by critics of the corporate world, is that since large corporations create many social problems, they should attempt to address and solve them. Those holding this view criticize the production, marketing, accounting, and environmental practices of corporations. They suggest that corporations can do a better job of producing quality, safe products by conducting their operations in an open and honest manner.

A very different argument in favor of corporate social responsibility is the self-interest argument. This is a long-term perspective that suggests corporations should conduct themselves in the present in a manner that ensures a promising operating environment in the future. Therefore, companies must look beyond the short-term benefits and the bottom-line perspective and recognize that investments in society today will be beneficial in the future. Furthermore, it may be in the corporate world's best interests to engage in socially responsive activities because, by doing so, the corporate world may forestall governmental intervention in the form of new legislation and regulation, according to Carroll and Buchholtz.

Finally, some suggest that businesses should assume social responsibilities because they are among the few private entities that have the resources to do so. The corporate world has some of the brightest minds in the world, and it possesses tremendous financial resources. (Walmart, for example, has annual revenues that exceed the annual GNP of some countries.) Thus, businesses should utilize some of their human and financial capital in order to "make the world a better place."

Contemporary Social Issues

Corporations deal with a wide variety of social issues and problems, some directly related to their operations, some not. It would not be possible to adequately describe all of the social issues faced by businesses. This section will briefly discuss three contemporary issues that are of major concern: the environment, global issues, and technology issues. There are many others.

Environmental Issues

Corporations have long been criticized for their negative effect on the natural environment in terms of wasting natural resources and contributing to environmental problems such as pollution and global warming. There is both governmental and societal pressure on corporations to adhere to stricter environmental standards and to voluntarily change production processes in order to do less harm to the environment. Other issues related to the natural environment include waste disposal, deforestation, acid rain, and land degradation. It is likely that corporate responsibilities in this area will increase in the coming years.

Global Issues

Corporations increasingly operate in a global environment. Critics suggest that globalization leads to the exploitation of developing nations and workers, destruction of the environment, and increased human rights abuses. They also argue that globalization primarily benefits the wealthy and widens the gap between the rich and the poor. Proponents of globalization argue that open markets lead to increased standards of living for everyone, higher wages for workers worldwide, and economic development in impoverished nations. Many large corporations are multinational in scope and will continue to face legal, social, and ethical issues brought on by the increasing globalization of business. Another issue in global business is the issue of marketing goods and services in the international marketplace. Some U.S. companies, for example, have marketed products in other countries after the products were banned in the United States.

Technology Issues

The Internet has opened up many new avenues for marketing goods and services, but it has also opened up the possibility of abuse by corporations. Issues of privacy and the security of confidential information must be addressed. The biotechnology industry also faces questions related to the use of embryonic stem cells, genetic engineering, and cloning. All of these issues have far-reaching societal and ethical implications. As technological capabilities continue to advance, it is likely that the responsibilities of corporations in this area will increase dramatically.

Corporate social responsibility is a complex topic. There is no question that the legal, ethical, and discretionary expectations placed on businesses are greater than ever before. Few companies totally disregard social issues and problems. Most purport to pursue not only the goal of increased revenues and profits, but also the goal of community and societal betterment.

Research suggests that those corporations that develop a reputation as being socially responsive and ethical enjoy higher levels of performance. However, the ultimate motivation for corporations to practice social responsibility should not be a financial motivation, but a moral and ethical one.

Sustainable Development

Similar to the concept of corporate social responsibility, the concept of sustainable development is present in discussions about economic development and the environment. However, this was not always the case. In 1972, Donella Meadows, Dennis Meadows, Jørgen Randers, and William Behrens, III, published their well-known book titled *Limits to Growth* in which they demonstrated that population and economic growth increase exponentially but are limited by the resources available. When this concept was presented, the idea of sustainable development was unknown. However, in retrospect, what the authors described in their book was the early alarm that initiated the drive for sustainable development (Meadows, Meadows, Randers, & Behrens, III, 1972).

It was only after the 1972 United Nations Conference on the Human Environment in Stockholm when the terms *environmentally sound development* or *eco-development* began to be used more frequently and sustainability gained popularity. Although back in the 1970s these concepts were not accurately defined, it was obvious that the type of development implied by the terms eco-development and sustainable development was different from the type of development discussed until then (Daly, 1997).

In the 1980s, the first major breakthrough in conceptual insight came from the formulation of the *World Conservation Strategy* by the International Union for Conservation of Nature (IUCN), the World Wildlife Fund (WWF), and the United Nations Environment Program (UNEP; IUCN, 1980). The integration of the strategic element of time within the context of the environment and development debate provided a platform that allowed for the addition of a range of issues such as efficiency, distribution of equity, conservation, resource management, and intergenerational responsibility that had not been included before.

In the late 1980s, the term sustainable development began to gain wide acceptance after its appearance in a document called *Our Common Future*, also known as the *Brundtland Report* published in 1987 by the Brundtland Commission (or the World Commission on Environment and Development [WCED]). This report is considered to be the milestone that started the process of rethinking the established ways of living and governing by introducing the idea that sustainable development can be achieved through governance and society's involvement. In addition, some economic, technological, social, and political prerequisites for sustainable development were identified. The report also provided the most commonly accepted definition of sustainable development: "sustainable development is development that meets the needs of the present without compromising the ability of future generations to meet their own needs" (Brundtland, 1987; Daly, 1997; Trzyna, 1995; WCED, 1987).

The strength of the sustainable development concept is that it reflects a change in the vision of how the economic activities of human beings relate to a finite environment. A condition of sustainable development is that the regeneration of raw materials and the absorption of waste are kept at ecologically sustainable levels. In other words, the regeneration and waste absorption of resources should be in equilibrium. This shift of thought involves the replacement of the standard economic quantitative measures of expansion, such as economic growth, with qualitative societal and environmental norms as the way to move forward. However, this shift is resisted by most economic and political institutions, which are founded on traditional quantitative growth (Brundtland, 1987; Trzyna, 1995).

At the macro level, sustainable development is commonly divided into three principal components also known as the triple bottom line (TBL) (Pope, Annandale, & Morrison-Saunders, 2004):

1. Economic growth
2. Social equity
3. Protection of the environment

The basis of the economic component is the principle that the well-being of a society has to be maximized and poverty has to be eradicated through the efficient use of natural resources (Redclift, 1987). The social component deals with the relationship of the society with the economy and the environment. Such a relationship is very broad and includes issues such as the welfare of people, the access to basic health and education services, minimum standards of security, and respect for human rights. It also refers to the development of various cultures, diversity, and pluralism. The issue of equitable distribution of benefits and access to resources is an essential component of both the economic and social dimensions of sustainable development.

The environmental component is concerned with the conservation and enhancement of the physical and biological resource base and ecosystems. The three sustainability components—economic, social, and environmental—are better tackled separately. The definition and main characteristics of each sustainability dimension are contrasted in the summary presented in Table 10.2. While there is some overlap among the three dimensions, different disciplines better address each one of them separately.

TABLE 10.2 Comparison of Social, Economic and Environmental Sustainability

Social Sustainability	Economic Sustainability	Environmental Sustainability
Definition		
Achieved by systematic community participation and strong civil society.	Achieved by maintenance of capital.	Achieved by maintaining natural capital.
Characteristics		
Social cohesion, cultural identity, diversity, etc. constitute a part of social capital. This human capital requires maintenance and replenishment. Investments in the education, health and nutrition of individuals are now accepted as part of economic development.	Seeks the maintenance of capital. Economists prefer to value things in monetary terms, therefore valuing correctly natural capital, intangible, intergenerational, and common-access resources such as air is crucial in order to measure economic sustainability.	Seeks to improve human welfare by protecting resources of raw materials used for human needs and ensuring that waste emissions are held within the assimilative capacity of the environment without impairing it.

Source: Adapted from (Goodland & Daly, 1996)

The concept of sustainable development has also shifted the perspective of how governments should make policies. Governments have the complex task of finding the appropriate balance between the competing demands on natural and social resources without slowing down economic progress. Since the economic, social, and environmental aspects of any actions are interconnected, they have to be considered in an integral manner. It is especially important to consider only one of these dimensions at a time to avoid errors in judgment and unsustainable outcomes. For example, the focus on profit margins only has historically led to social and environmental damages that in the long term end up costing society. Similarly, taking care of the environment and the ability to provide social services depends a great deal on economic resources. The interconnected and interdependent nature of sustainable development also requires thinking beyond geographical and institutional borders in order to coordinate strategies and make good decisions (Strange & Bayley, 2008).

Sustainability Assessment

There is an ongoing debate about sustainability assessments. However, according to some scholars, the consensus about sustainability assessments is that any sound assessment should include the following:

- Integrate economic, environmental, social, and institutional issues as well as their interconnections.
- Consider the consequences of current actions far into the futu
- Recognize the uncertainty regarding the results of current actions.
- Engage the public.
- Incorporate intragenerational and intergenerational considerations. (Gasparatos, El-Haram, & Horner, 2007)

The challenge of making sustainable development operational is the ability to evaluate and manage at a macro level the complex interrelationships among economic, social, and environmental objectives. At the United Nations Conference on Environment and Development in 1992, documents that outlined a plan and the principles to achieve sustainable development were put forward. These documents are known as the Agenda and the Rio Declaration. The Agenda and the Declaration had a wide range of initiatives that brought the sustainability concept closer to being an operational guide for assessing sustainability (Agenda 21, 1993; Dernbach, 1998).

Nowadays sustainability assessment is increasingly viewed as an important tool to aid in the widespread shift toward sustainability. However, this is a new and evolving concept and there are few examples of effective sustainability assessment processes implemented so far.

Sustainability assessment is often described as the process in which the implications of an initiative on sustainability are evaluated (Spangenberg, Omann, & Hinterberger, 2002). This generic definition includes a broad range of different processes. Many of the existing assessment frameworks are examples of integrated assessments directly derived from the Strategic Environmental Assessment (SEA), the Sustainability Impact Assessment (SIA), and the Environmental Impact Assessment (EIA) frameworks that incorporate economic, environmental, and social considerations. This approach is also known as a Triple Bottom Line (TBL) approach to sustainability that we discussed previously. These integrated assessment processes usually either try to find ways to minimize unsustainability, or attempt to achieve TBL objectives (Gasparatos et al., 2007; Jansen, 2003; Pope et al., 2004).

The major conclusions regarding sustainability assessment frameworks can be summarized as follows:

- Sustainability assessments must assess the sustainability of an initiative in addition to assessing the final outcome.
- Societal goals should be conceptually clear.

In order to measure the progress toward sustainable development, it is necessary to identify operational indicators that provide manageable and accurate information on economic, environmental, and social conditions. Since the early 1990s, many indicators have been developed. The compendium of sustainable development indicators lists more than 500 sustainable indicators (Parris & Kates, 2003).

Böhringer and Jochem (2007) reviewed 11 sustainable development indices and studied their consistency and meaningfulness. They concluded that the indicators listed in Table 10.3 are concise and transparent, but that they do not appropriately use fundamental scientific requirements such as the technical aggregation method, the normalization of variables and their weighting, as well as the commensurability of input variables (Böhringer & Jochem, 2007).

The general conclusion about sustainability indicators and indices is that they can be powerful tools, but only if they are used appropriately. Even though the methods used for assessing the consistency and transparency of these indicators is relatively objective, a certain subjective bias is bound to

TABLE 10.3   Sustainable Development Indices

Acronym	Sustainable Development Indicator
EF	Ecological Footprint
HDI	Human Development Index
ESI	Environmental Sustainability Index
EPI	Environmental Performance Index
EVI	Environmental Vulnerability Index
EDP	Environmental Adjusted Domestic Product
LPI	Living Planet Index
CDI	City Development Index
WI	Well-Being Index
ISEW/GPI	Index of Sustainable Economic Welfare/Genuine Progress Index
GS	Genuine Savings Index

exist. Composite indicators may give ambiguous and unreliable information if they are poorly constructed or misinterpreted. The lack of a clear understanding of how the indicators are developed and what information they convey is critical for policymaking decisions using such indicators. The incorrect interpretation of indexes and indicators may result in flawed policy decisions that could lead to the increase of economic disparities, promote environmental damage, and even decrease the possibilities for long-term sustainability (Golusin & Munitlak Ivanovic, 2009; Mayer, 2008; Siche, Agostinho, Ortega, & Romeiro, 2008; Singh, Murty, Gupta, & Dikshit, 2009).

As a standard practice, any policies and development activities ought to be monitored and evaluated to determine whether the policies or activities need adjustment or whether they should be eliminated altogether. In addition, the monitoring and evaluation would facilitate the identification and verification of the appropriate sustainability indicators that should be used for policy decision making. Finally, the monitoring should be continuous to determine both the short-term and the long-term cumulative and synergistic effects.

Environmental Sustainability

The World Bank's definition of environmental sustainability is, "Ensuring that the overall productivity of accumulated human and physical capital resulting from development actions more than compensates for the direct or indirect loss or degradation of the environment." (Agenda 21, 1993). This is the starting point of all the existing indicators that measure environmental sustainability as well as the basis of many governmental policies and firm level initiatives.

The World Bank Group's mandate calls for the reduction of poverty and the improvement of the lives of people. This mandate is very closely linked to the need of dealing with environmental degradation and guaranteeing environmental sustainability. One of the goals set at the UN Millennium Development Goals (Goal 7) specifically refers to the integration of the principles of sustainable development into country policies and programs to reverse and prevent the loss of environmental resources (World Bank, 2010).

The measurement and valuation of natural capital or the environment is one of the many difficulties in applying the sustainability concept. Despite these difficulties, it is clear that the protection of the environment is an essential dimension of sustainable development. Some of the environmental challenges, such as water scarcity, and environmental degradation should be handled at national and regional levels to ensure the sustainable development of a country or region.

Oftentimes it is easier to deal with environmental sustainability in terms of environmental unsustainability. We tend to be more familiar with the undesired outcomes than with the desired ones. Table 10.4 summarizes the symptoms of environmental unsustainability and their causes (Ekins, 2000).

TABLE 10.4   Symptoms of "Environmental Unsustainability" and Their Causes

Problem	Principal Agents
Pollution	
Greenhouse effect/Climate change (global)	Emissions of CO_2, N_2O, CH_4, CFCs (and
Acidification (continental)	HFCs), O_3 (low lever), PFCs, SF_x, SO_2,
Toxic Contamination	NO_x, NH_3, O_3 (low level), Particulates, heavy metals, hydrocarbons, CO, agrochemicals, organo-chlorides, eutrophiers, radiation, noise.
Renewable Resource Depletion	
Species extinction (global)	Land use changes (e.g., development,
Deforestation	deforestation, population pressure,
Land degradation/loss of soil fertility	unsustainable harvest, climate change,
Water Depletion	ozone depletion.)
Fishery destruction	Overfishing, destructive technologies, pollution, habitat destruction.
Non-Renewable Resource Depletion	
Depletion of various resources	Extraction and use of fossil fuels, minerals.

Source: Adapted from P. Ekins (2000)

Criteria for Environmental Sustainability

Organizations such as the Organisation for Economic Co-operation and Development (OECD), the United Nations Department of Economic and Social Affairs (UNDESA), the World Bank, the Organization of American States (OAS), and many others are continuously developing measurements and methods to assess programs, projects, and investment strategies based on an environmental sustainability approach. Specific indicators of environmental sustainability are usually used in such methods and assessments. The understanding and ability of managing renewable resources in the long term is crucial to the implementation of any environmental sustainable initiatives. Such initiatives should significantly reduce waste and pollution, use energy and materials effectively and efficiently, and invest in repairing the industrialization damage in many parts of the world. In order to achieve environmental sustainability, enabling conditions that are not usually considered to be integral parts of environmental sustainability must be included. Such enabling conditions are democracy, continuous human resource development, and investment in human capital.

According to Goodland and Daly (1996) and other scholars, the basic condition for environmental sustainability is the maintenance of nonsubstitutable, nonrenewable natural resources. This means that there cannot be net increases in waste emissions beyond the absorptive capacity (Redwood, Eerikainen, & Tarazona, 2008; Spangenberg et al., 2002; Stinchcombe & Gibson, 2001; Ulhoi & Madsen, 1999).

Country Level Sustainability

Environmental issues are many and far reaching, and this chapter does not seek to address the entire scope of the subject. However, as economic integration increases, what happens in one country or in an economically integrated region often impacts other countries or economically integrated regions.

The United Nations Development Programme (UNDP) created the Human Development Index (HDI). This is a composite index widely used to measure the development of a nation or a city. The index combines conditions of longevity, health, education, and economic well-being of a population to determine a measure of "human development." The HDI is commonly used as a proxy metric to measure the progress toward human development goals. Specifically, the HDI of a country is a combination of four dimensions: life expectancy at birth, adult literacy rate, and gross school enrollment ratio and GNI per capita (PPP US$; UNDP, 2010). The

HDI is often used as a complementary metric to more traditional indicators that purely reflects economic development, such as the GDP.

The HDI scale is from 0.0 to 1.0. A higher value of HDI indicates that a country has achieved high values for each subindex, and a low value indicates that the country has low values for all subindices. The United Nations Development Programme (UNDP) provides a ranking of countries according to their HDI scores. An HDI score of 0.80 is the limit between medium and high human development. In other words, countries with an HDI score of 0.80 or higher are considered to have high human development. Countries with HDI scores below 0.80 are considered to have medium to low human development.

One of the criticisms of the HDI is that it does not include an environmental component. Since human development affects the biosphere through the use of its resources and services, the HDI alone is not sufficient to determine environmentally sustainable development. A necessary condition of environmental sustainability is that the waste generated by humans is converted back into resources at the same time in order to keep the equilibrium. The current situation is not in equilibrium because waste is generated faster than the biosphere's capacity to absorb and regenerate the waste. If human activity overburdens the biosphere's regenerative capacities, the waste accumulates and the natural capital is depleted. Therefore, the use of resources for human development will be sustainable only if the demands for natural resources remain within the regenerative capacity of the earth. The Ecological Footprint (EF) is an index that measures the regenerative capacity of the biosphere used by human activities. By determining the area of biologically productive land and water required to support a population at its current level of consumption the so-called "footprint" is calculated. Thus, a country's Ecological Footprint is the total area required to produce everything a population consumes, absorb the waste it generates, and provide area for its infrastructure. If reductions in resource use are achieved (either through decreasing consumption or by improving efficiency of production) the Ecological Footprint per capita would be reduced. In contrast to the Ecological Footprint index which addresses the demand on ecosystems, the Biocapacity measures the productive capacity of the biosphere and its ability to provide a flux of biological resources and services useful to humanity (footprintnetwork.org, 2014).

Both the Ecological Footprint index and the Biocapacity are measured in global hectares. A global hectare represents a hectare of land with world average bioproductivity. According to Daniel D. Moran, Mathis Wackernagel, Justin A. Kitzes, Steven H. Goldfinger and Aurelie Boutaud (2008), the comparison of the Ecological Footprint index to the Biocapacity can provide a useful indicator of ecological sustainability.

A large body of literature has examined the strengths and shortcomings of the Ecological Footprint approach (Chambers, 2001; Kitzes et al., 2009; Monfreda, Wackernagel, & Deumling, 2004). Yet despite acknowledged limitations, the Ecological Footprint is one of the most commonly used biophysical indicators for comparing present aggregate human demand on the biosphere with the Earth's gross ecological capacity to sustain human life. The Ecological Footprint index primarily uses UN statistics that are complemented with data publicly available.

Moran et al. (2008) propose in their paper that the sustainable development of nations can be examined in terms of two dimensions: the UNDP Human Development Index (HDI) as an indicator of development and the Ecological Footprint to the Biocapacity ratio as an indicator of human demand on the biosphere. Using these two dimensions, they assessed the sustainable development of 93 nations. In addition, they argue that an HDI of no less than 0.8 (HDI0.8) and an Ecological Footprint to the Biocapacity ratio of less than 1.0 (EF/Biocapacity1.0) is the minimum requirement for environmentally sustainable development that is globally replicable. They found in their study that despite increased global adoption of sustainable development policies, only a few of the 93 countries surveyed in their study met both of these minimum requirements (Moran, Wackernagel, Kitzes, Goldfinger, & Boutaud, 2008).

Sustainability at the Firm Level

The Global Reporting Initiative (GRI) is a network-based organization that pioneered the world's most widely used sustainability reporting framework (GRI, 2014). The core goal of the Global Reporting Initiative framework is that the disclosure of a company's economic, environmental, and social performance becomes a widely accepted standard practice.

The GRI provides a reporting framework that outlines the principles and performance indicators that organizations should use to measure and report their economic, environmental, and social performance. A sustainability report based on the GRI framework is expected to provide a relatively accurate picture of the sustainability performance of the reporting organization. In addition, the report is supposed to be somewhat balanced because it includes both the positive and the negative contributions of the organization.

The sustainability reports created based on this framework are required to disclose the outcomes and results that occur within the reporting period.

Usually that reporting period is a year. Since different companies and organizations follow the same framework and the reports cover a particular period, these reports can be very useful in benchmarking and assessing the sustainability performance with respect to voluntary initiatives, performance standards, norms, codes, and laws. In addition, the organization's performance can be tracked over time as well as compared with other organizations and companies in a similar category.

One of the advantages of the GRI reporting framework is that it applies to any size company and it is independent of the location and the sector of the company. In other words, small companies can use the framework, as well as companies with geographically dispersed operations.

GRI Reporting Framework Dimensions

Economic dimension: The economic dimension of the framework takes into account the impacts of a company on the economic systems at local, national, and global levels, as well as the impact on the economic conditions of its stakeholders. Some of the economic indicators in this dimension include the flow of capital. Financial performance is crucial to understanding the sustainability contribution of an organization to the larger economic system.

Environmental dimension: The environmental sustainability of a firm is determined by the firm's impact on the natural systems where the company operates. These include living and nonliving ecosystems. Environmental indicators used in the framework are related to the performance of the inputs relative to the outputs. In addition, it includes measures that indicate the level of environmental compliance with the laws and regulations of the company, as well as indicators that measure the impact of the company's products and services on biodiversity (see Table 10.5).

Social dimension: The indicators used to determine the company's sustainability performance in the social dimension measure aspects related to labor practices, education, product responsibility, and human rights.

To encourage the use of the GRI framework to address environmental sustainability concerns, we need to create a positive loop that connects a firm's environmental sustainability to the performance of the firm. If this positive relationship is developed, the firm will improve its performance and practice an environmentally friendly behavior at the same time. One way to develop this positive relationship is to encourage buyers to consider the environmental aspect of the firm as criteria to choose a product.

TABLE 10.5   GRI Environmental Performance Indicators

Aspect	Indicator
Materials	• Materials used by weight or volume. • Percentage of materials used that are recycled input materials.
Energy	• Direct energy consumption by primary energy source. • Indirect energy consumption by primary source. • Energy saved due to conservation and efficiency improvements. • Initiatives to provide energy-efficient or renewable energy based products and services, and reductions in energy requirements as a result of these initiatives. • Initiatives to reduce indirect energy consumption and reductions achieved.
Water	• Total water withdrawal by source. • Water sources significantly affected by withdrawal of water. • Percentage and total volume of water recycled and reused.
Biodiversity	• Location and size of land owned, leased, managed in, or adjacent to, protected areas and areas of high biodiversity value outside protected areas. • Description of significant impacts of activities, products, and services on biodiversity in protected areas and areas of high biodiversity value outside-protected areas. • Habitats protected or restored. • Strategies, current actions, and future plans for managing impacts on biodiversity. • Number of IUCN Red List species and national conservation list species with habitats in areas affected by operations, by level of extinction risk.
Emissions, Effluents, and Waste	• Total direct and indirect greenhouse gas emissions by weight. • Other relevant indirect greenhouse gas emissions by weight. • Initiatives to reduce greenhouse gas emissions and reductions achieved. • Emissions of ozone-depleting substances by weight. • NO, SO, and other significant air emissions by type and weight. • Total water discharge by quality and destination. • Total weight of waste by type and disposal method. • Total number and volume of significant spills. • Weight of transported, imported, exported, or treated waste deemed hazardous, and percentage of transported waste shipped internationally. • Identity, size, protected status, and biodiversity value of water bodies and related habitats significantly affected by the reporting organization's discharges of water and runoff.

Source: Adapted from GRI website (http://www.globalreporting.org/Home)

References

Adams, J. S., Tashchian, A., & Shore, T. H. (2001). Codes of ethics as signals for ethical behavior. *Journal of Business Ethics, 29*(3), 199–211.

Agenda 21, (1993). *The United Nations programme of action from Rio de Janeiro.* New York, NY: UN Department of Public Information.

Appleyard, D., Field, A., & Cobb, S. (2010). *International Economics* (7th ed.). New York, NY: McGraw-Hill.

Asgary, N., & Li, G. (2014). Corporate social responsibility: Its economic impact and link to the bullwhip effect. *Journal of Business Ethics, 81*(1), 223–234.

Asgary, N., & Mitschow, M. C. (2002). Toward a model for international business ethics. *Journal of Business Ethics, 36*(3), 239–246.

Barney, J. B. (1997). *Gaining and sustaining competitive advantage* (P. Education ed.). Reading, MA: Addison-Wesley.

BBC News. (2010). EU ministers offer 750bn-euro plan to support currency. Retrieved August 16, 2014, from http://news.bbc.co.uk/2/hi/business/8671632.stm

Benedict, R. (1989). *Patterns of culture.* Boston, MA: Mariner Books.

Bennear, L. S., & Stavins, R. N. (2007). Second-best theory and the use of multiple policy instruments. *Environmental and Resource Economics, 37*(1), 111–129.

Bhagwati, J. N. (1998). The capital myth: The difference between trade in widgets and dollars. *Foreign Affairs, 77,* 7–12.

Bhagwati, J. N., Panagariya, A., & Srinivasan, T. N. (1998). *Lectures on international trade.* Cambridge, MA: MIT Press.

BIS. (2014). *Basel Committee on banking supervision.* Retrieved August 11, 2014, from http://www.bis.org/bcbs/

Foundations of Global Business, pages 159–167

Blomstrom, M., & Kokko, A. (1997). *Regional integration and foreign direct investment.* NBER working paper.

Böhringer, C., & Jochem, P. E. P. (2007). Measuring the immeasurable: A survey of sustainability indices. *Ecological Economics, 63*(1), 1–8. doi: 10.1016/j. ecolecon.2007.03.008

Brundtland, G. (1987). *World commission on environment and development: Our common future.* Oxford, England: Oxford University Press.

Buchholtz, A. K., & Carroll, A. B. (2012). *Business & society: Ethics & stakeholder management.* Boston, MA: South-Western Cengage Learning.

Buckley, P. J., & Casson, M. (1976). *The future of the multinational enterprise* (Vol. 1). London, England: Macmillan.

Buckley, P. J., & Casson, M. C. (1998). Analyzing foreign market entry strategies: Extending the internalization approach. *Journal of International Business Studies, 29,* 539–561.

Buckley, P. J., & Casson, M. C. (2009). The internalisation theory of the multinational enterprise: A review of the progress of a research agenda after 30 years. *Journal of International Business Studies, 40*(9), 1563–1580.

Buckley, P. J., & Ghauri, P. N. (2004). Globalisation, economic geography and the strategy of multinational enterprises. *Journal of International Business Studies, 35*(2), 81–98.

Byrnes, S. J. (2007, Fall). Balancing investor rights and environmental protection investor-state dispute settlement under CAFTA: Lessons from the NAFTA legitimacy crisis. *Business Law Journal, University of California Davis, 8,* 102.

Cairncross, F. (2001). *The death of distance: How the communications revolution is changing our lives.* Boston, MA: Harvard Business Press.

Calame, P. (2008, June). *Non-state actors, due to their vocation, size, flexibility, methods of organization and action, interact with states on a level playing field.* Retrieved August 16, 2014, from http://www.world-governance.org/spip. php?article273

Chambers, G. (Ed.). (2001). Ecological footprinting: A technical report to the STOA panel. Published by European Parliament, Directorate General for Research, Directorate A, The SOTA Programme.

Clark, D. (2009). Adjustment problems in developing countries and the U.S.-Central America-Dominican Republic Free Trade Agreement. *The International Trade Journal, 23*(1), 31–53.

Coase, R. H. (1937). The nature of the firm. *Economica, 4*(16), 386–405.

Coase, R. H. (1988, Spring). The nature of the firm: Influence. *Journal of Law, Economics, & Organization, (4)*1, 33–47.

Cosset, J.-C., & Roy, J. (1991). The determinants of country risk ratings. *Journal of International Business Studies, (22)*1, 135–142.

Daly, H. (1997). *Beyond growth: The economics of sustainable development.* Boston, MA Beacon Press.

Daniels, J., Radebaugh, L. & Sullivan, D. (2007). *International business: Environments and operations* (11th ed.). Upper Saddle River, NJ: Prentice Hall.

Dernbach, J. (1998). Sustainable development as a framework for national governance. *Case Western Reserve Law Review, 49*(1).

Drezner, D. W. (2001). Globalization and policy convergence. *International Studies Review, 3*(1), 53–78.

Dunning, J. H. (1976). *Trade, location of economic activity and the MNE: A search for an eclectic approach.* Berkshire, England: University of Reading, Department of Economics.

Dunning, J. H. (1979). Explaining changing patterns of international production: In defence of the eclectic theory. *Oxford Bulletin of Economics and Statistics, 41*(4), 269–295.

Dunning, J. H. (1993, March). Internationalizing Porter's diamond. *MIR: Management International Review, 33*(2-1), 7–15.

Dunning, J. H. (2001). The eclectic (OLI) paradigm of international production: Past, present and future. *International Journal of the Economics of Business, 8*(2), 173–190.

Dunning, J. H. (2009). Location and the multinational enterprise: John Dunning's thoughts on receiving the Journal of International Business Studies 2008 Decade Award. *Journal of International Business Studies, 40*(1), 20–34.

Dunning, J. H., Van Hoesel, R., & Narula, R. 1997. Third world multinationals revisited: New developments and theoretical implications. In J. H. Dunning (Ed.), *Globalization, trade and foreign direct investment* (pp. 255–286). Oxford, England: Pergammon Press.

Ekins, P. (2000). *Economic growth and environmental sustainability: The prospects for green growth.* New York, NY: Routledge.

Footprintnetwork.org. (2014). *Footprint for nations.* Retrieved August 16, 2014, from http://www.footprintnetwork.org/en/index.php/GFN/page/footprint_for_nations/

Fowler, H. W., & Fowler, F. G. (2011). *The concise Oxford dictionary: The classic first edition.* Oxford, England: Oxford University Press.

Freeman, R. E. (2010). *Strategic management: A stakeholder approach.* New York, NY: Cambridge University Press. Originally published in 1984.

Friedman, T. L. (2000). *The Lexus and the olive tree: Understanding globalization.* London, England: Macmillan.

FTI. (2014). *Fairtrade International.* Retrieved August 11, 2014, from http://www.fairtrade.net/

Fukao, K., Okubo, T., & Stern, R. M. (2003). An econometric analysis of trade diversion under NAFTA. *The North American Journal of Economics and Finance, 14*(1), 3–24.

Gasparatos, A., El-Haram, M., & Horner, M. (2007). A critical review of reductionist approaches for assessing the progress towards sustainability. *Environmental Impact Assessment Review, 28*(4/5), 286–311. doi: 10.1016/j.eiar.2007.09.002

Geertz, C. (1973). *The interpretation of cultures* (pp. 412–453). New York, NY: Basic.

Ghemawat, P. (2001). Distance still matters. *Harvard Business Review, 79*(8), 137–147.

Golusin, M., & Munitlak Ivanovic, O. (2009). Definition, characteristics and state of the indicators of sustainable development in countries of Southeastern Europe. *Agriculture, Ecosystems & Environment, 130*(1/2), 67–74. doi: 10.1016/j.agee.2008.11.018

Goodland, R., & Daly, H. (1996). Environmental sustainability: Universal and non-negotiable. *Ecological Applications, 6*(4), 1002–1017.

GRI. (2014). *Reporting principles and standard disclosures.* Retrieved January 7, 2014, from https://www.globalreporting.org/reporting/Pages/default.aspx

Haier.com. (2014). *Haier Group Chairman & CEO, Zhang Ruimin, ranked among "The world's 50 greatest leaders."* Retrieved April 9, 2014, from http://www.haier.com/uk/newspress/pressreleases/201404/t20140409_216131.shtml

Hamel, G. (1991). Competition for competence and interpartner learning within international strategic alliances. *Strategic Management Journal, 12*(Summer Special Issue), 83–103.

Hamel, G., & Prahalad, C. K. (1985). Do you really have a global strategy? *Harvard Business Review, 63*(4), 139–148.

Hamel, I. (2006). *Fair trade firm accused of foul play: SWI swissinfo.ch.* Retrieved August 16, 2014, from http://www.swissinfo.ch/eng/fair-trade-firm-accused-of-foul-play/5351232

Heller, H. R. (1968). International trade; theory and empirical evidence. Englewood Cliffs, N.J., Prentice-Hall.

Hempel, J. (2011). IBM's Sam Palmisano: A super second act. *Fortune tech: Technology blogs, news and analysis.* Retrieved August 16, 2014, from http://fortune.com/2011/03/04/ibms-sam-palmisano-a-super-second-act/

Hoad, T. F. (1993). *The concise Oxford dictionary of English etymology.* Oxford, England: Oxford University Press.

Hofstede, G. (1984). *Culture's consequences: International differences in work-related values* (Vol. 5). Thousand Oaks, CA: Sage.

Hornbeck, J. (2005a). *The Dominican Republic-Central America-United States Free Trade Agreement (CAFTA-DR).* CRS Report for Congress.

Hornbeck, J. (2005b). The U.S.-Central America Free Trade Agreement (CAFTA): Challenges for sub-regional integration. *Congressional Research Service Report.*

IMF. (2000). Transition economies: An IMF perspective on progress and prospects. *Issues Briefs.* Retrieved August 16, 2014, from http://www.imf.org/external/np/exr/ib/2000/110300.htm#I

IMF. (2014). *International Monetary Fund* [Home page]. Retrieved August 11, 2014, from http://www.imf.org/external/index.htm

IUCN. (1980). *World conservation strategy: Living resource conservation for sustainable development.* Retrieved from https://portals.iucn.org/library/efiles/html/WCS-004/cover.html

Jansen, L. (2003). The challenge of sustainable development. *Journal of Cleaner Production, 11*(3), 231–245.

Johanson, J., & Vahlne, J.-E. (1977). The internationalization process of the firm: A model of knowledge development and increasing foreign market commitments. *Journal of International Business Studies, 8*, 23–32. doi:10.1057/palgrave.jibs.8490676

Johanson, J., & Wiedersheim-Paul, F. (1975). The internationalization of the firm: Four Swedish cases 1. *Journal of Management Studies, 12*(3), 305–323.

Jones, R. J. B. (1995). *Globalisation and interdependence in the international political economy: rhetoric and reality.* London, England: Pinter.

Kettl, D. F. (2000). The transformation of governance: Globalization, devolution, and the role of government. *Public Administration Review, 60*(6), 488–497.

Kitzes, J., Galli, A., Bagliani, M., Barrett, J., Dige, G., Ede, S., . . . Hails, C. (2009). A research agenda for improving national Ecological Footprint accounts. *Ecological Economics, 68*(7), 1991–2007.

Kluckhohn, F., & Strodtbeck, F. L. (1961). *Variations in value orientation.* Evanston, IL: Row, Peterson.

Krugman, P., & Wells, R. (2012). *Macroeconomics* (3rd ed.). New York, NY: Worth.

Kwok, C. C. Y., & Reeb, D. M. (2000). Internationalization and firm risk: An upstream-downstream hypothesis. *Journal of International Business Studies, 31*(4), 611–629.

Lane, H. W., Maznevski, M., Dietz, J., & DiStefano, J. J. (2009). *International management behavior: Leading with a global mindset.* Hoboken, NJ: Wiley.

Laplume, A. O., Sonpar, K., & Litz, R. A. (2008). Stakeholder theory: Reviewing a theory that moves us. *Journal of Management, 34*(6), 1152–1189.

Lin, J. Y., & Nugent, J. B. (1995). Institutions and economic development. In J. Behrman & T. N. Srinivasan (Eds.), *Handbook of development economics* (Vol. 3A). New York, NY: Elsevier Science.

Lipsey, R. G., & Lancaster, K. (1956). The general theory of second best. *The Review of Economic Studies, 24*(1), 11–32.

London, T., & Hart, S. L. (2010). *Next generation business strategies for the base of the pyramid: New approaches for building mutual value.* London, England: FT Press.

Lopez-De-Pedro, J. M., & Rimbau-Gilabert, E. (2012). Stakeholder approach: What effects should we take into account in contemporary societies? *Journal of Business Ethics, 107*(2), 147–158.

Mayer, A. L. (2008). Strengths and weaknesses of common sustainability indices for multidimensional systems. *Environment International, 34*(2), 277–291. doi: 10.1016/j.envint.2007.09.004

Meadows, D. H., Meadows, D. L., Randers, J., & Behrens, W. W., III (1972). *The limits to growth: A report for the Club of Rome's project on the predicament of mankind.* New York, NY: Universe Books.

Meier, G. M. (1968). *The international economics of development. Theory and policy.* New Delhi, India: Harper & Row.

Monfreda, C., Wackernagel, M., & Deumling, D. (2004). Establishing national natural capital accounts based on detailed ecological footprint and biological capacity assessments. *Land Use Policy, 21*(3), 231–246.

Monge-González, R., & González-Alvarado, C. (2007). The role and impact of MNCs in Costa Rica on skills development and training: The case of Intel, Microsoft and Cisco. *Report to the International Labor Organization.*

Moran, D. D., Wackernagel, M., Kitzes, J. A., Goldfinger, S. H., & Boutaud, A. (2008). Measuring sustainable development: Nation by nation. *Ecological Economics, 64*(3), 470–474. doi: 10.1016/j.ecolecon.2007.08.017

Morecroft, J. (2007). *Strategic modelling and business dynamics: A feedback systems approach.* New York, NY: Wiley.

Munger, M. (2014). Forget Fairtrade Fortnight, let the market work. *Adam Smith Institute.* Retrieved August 11, 2014, from http://www.adamsmith.org/blog/tax-spending/forget-fairtrade-fortnight-let-the-market-work/

NIC. (2014). Eurasia. *National Intelligence Council.* Retrieved from http://www.dni.gov/index.php/about/organization/national-intelligence-council-nic-publications

OECD. (2014). *Transfer pricing.* Retrieved August 22, 2014, from http://www.oecd.org/ctp/transfer-pricing/

Pan, Y., & Tse, D. K. (2000). The hierarchical model of market entry modes. *Journal of International Business Studies,* 31(4), 535–554.

Parris, T. M., & Kates, R. W. (2003). Characterizing and measuring sustainable development. *Annual Review of Environment and Resources, 28,* 559–586.

Paunovic, I. (2005). *El tratado de libre comercio Centroamérica-Estados Unidos: Implicaciones fiscales para los países centroamericanos* (Vol. 34). Herndon, VA: United Nations Publications.

Peng, M. (2013). *Global strategy.* Boston, MA: Cengage Learning.

Peng, M. W. (2001). The resource-based view and international business. *Journal of Management, 27*(6), 803–829.

Peng, M. W. (2002). Towards an institution-based view of business strategy. *Asia Pacific Journal of Management, 19*(2/3), 251–267.

Peng, M. W., Wang, D. Y. L., & Jiang, Y. (2008). An institution-based view of international business strategy: A focus on emerging economies. *Journal of International Business Studies, 39*(5), 920–936.

Pope, J., Annandale, D., & Morrison-Saunders, A. (2004). Conceptualising sustainability assessment. *Environmental Impact Assessment Review, 24*(6), 595–616.

Porter, M. (1998). *Competitive strategy: Techniques for analyzing industries and competitors.* New York, NY: Free Press.

Porter, M. E. (1990). The competitive advantage of nations. *Harvard Business Review, 68*(2).

Porter, M. E. (1998a). Clusters and the new economics of competition. *Harvard Business Review, (76)*6.

Porter, M. E. (1998b). *Competing across locations: Enhancing competitive advantage through a global strategy.* Boston, MA: Harvard Business School Press.

Prahalad, C. K. (2009). *The fortune at the bottom of the pyramid, revised and updated* (5th anniversary ed.): *Eradicating poverty through profits.* Upper Saddle River, NJ: FT Press.

Redclift, M. (1987). *Sustainable development: Exploring the contradictions.* London, England: Routledge.

Redwood, J., Eerikainen, J., & Tarazona, E. (2008). *Environmental sustainability: An evaluation of World Bank Group support.* Washington, DC: The World Bank.

Reeb, D. M., Kwok, C. C. Y., & Baek, H. Y. (1998). Systematic risk of the multinational corporation. *Journal of International Business Studies, 29*(2), 263–279.

Ricart, J. E., Enright, M. J., Ghemawat, P., Hart, S. L., & Khanna, T. (2004). New frontiers in international strategy. *Journal of International Business Studies, 35*(3), 175–200.

Rodrik, D. (2008). *One economics, many recipes: Globalization, institutions, and economic growth.* Princeton, NJ: Princeton University Press.

Rugman, A. (2012). *The end of globalization.* New York, NY: Random House.

Rugman, A. M. (1980). Internalization as a general theory of foreign direct investment: A re-appraisal of the literature. *Review of World Economics, 116*(2), 365–379.

Rugman, A. M., & Verbeke, A. (2004). A perspective on regional and global strategies of multinational enterprises. *Journal of International Business Studies, 35*(1), 3–18.

Sachs, J. (2006). *The end of poverty: Economic possibilities for our time.* New York, NY: Penguin Press.

Samuelson, P. A. (1939). The gains from international trade. *The Canadian Journal of Economics and Political Science/Revue canadienne d'Economique et de Science politique, 5*(2), 195–205.

Samuelson, P. A. (1948). International trade and the equalisation of factor prices. *The Economic Journal, 58*(230), 163–184.

Senge, P. M. (2006). *The fifth discipline: The art and practice of the learning organization.* New York, NY: Random House.

Senge, P. M., Kleiner, A., Roberts, C., Ross, R., & Smith, B. (1994). *The fifth discipline fieldbook: Strategies and tools for building a learning organization.* New York, NY: Doubleday.

Sethi, S. P. (2005). Voluntary codes of conduct for multinational corporations. *Journal of Business Ethics, 59*(1), 1–2.

Sherwood, D. (2002). *Seeing the forest for the trees: A manager's guide to applying systems thinking.* Boston, MA: Nicholas Brealey.

Siche, J. R., Agostinho, F., Ortega, E., & Romeiro, A. (2008). Sustainability of nations by indices: Comparative study between environmental sustainability index, ecological footprint and the emergy performance indices. *Ecological Economics, 66*(4), 628–637. doi: 10.1016/j.ecolecon.2007.10.023

Singh, R. K., Murty, H. R., Gupta, S. K., & Dikshit, A. K. (2009). An overview of sustainability assessment methodologies. *Ecological Indicators, 9*(2), 189–212. doi: 10.1016/j.ecolind.2008.05.011

Spangenberg, J. H., Omann, I., & Hinterberger, F. (2002). Sustainable growth criteria: Minimum benchmarks and scenarios for employment and the environment. *Ecological Economics, 42*(3), 429–443.

Steers, R. M., Sanchez-Runde, C. J., & Nardon, L. (2010). *Management across cultures: Challenges and strategies.* Cambridge, England: Cambridge University Press.

Sterman, J. D. (2000). *Business dynamics: Systems thinking and modeling for a complex world* (Vol. 19). Boston, MA: Irwin/McGraw-Hill.

Stiglitz, J. E. (2003). *Globalization and its discontents.* New York, NY: W.W. Norton.

Stiglitz, J. E. (2007). *Making globalization work.* New York, NY: W.W. Norton.

Stinchcombe, K., & Gibson, R. B. (2001). Strategic environmental assessment as a means of pursuing sustainability. *Journal of Environmental Assessment Policy and Management, 3*(3), 343–372.

Strange, T., & Bayley, A. (2008). *Sustainable development: Linking economy, society, environment.* Paris, France: OECD Publishing.

Subway.com. (2014). *The history of Subway.* Retrieved August 16, 2014, from http://franchise.subway.com/subwayroot/about_us/history.aspx

Trzyna, T. (1995). *A sustainable world: Defining and measuring sustainable development.* Sacramento, CA: Published for IUCN, the World Conservation Union by the International Center for the Environment and Public Policy.

Ulhoi, J. P., & Madsen, H. (1999). *Sustainable development and sustainable growth: Conceptual plain or points on a conceptual plain?* Retrieved at http://www.systemdynamics.org/conferences/1999/PAPERS/PARA197.PDF

UNDP. (2010). Human development index. *Human Development Reports.* Retrieved from http://hdr.undp.org/en/statistics/indices/

UNESCO. (2002). *UNESCO World Heritage Centre–World Heritage.* Retrieved from http://whc.unesco.org/en/about/

USTR. (2005, February). CAFTA-facts: Free trade with Central America and the Dominican Republic. *Office of the United States Trade Representative.* Retrieved from https://ustr.gov/archive/assets/Trade_Agreements/Regional/CAFTA/Briefing_Book/asset_upload_file834_7179.pdf

Vernon, R. (1966). International investment and international trade in the product cycle. *The Quarterly Journal of Economics, 80*(2), 190–207.

WCED: World Commission on Environment and Development. (1987). *Our common future.* Oxford, England: Oxford University Press.

Wipro. (2014). *2014.* Retrieved from http://www.wipro.com/

World Bank Group. (2014). Retrieved from http://www.worldbank.org/

World Bank. (2010). *The World Bank and the environment.* Retrieved from http://www.worldbank.org/en/topic/environment

WTO. (2004). *Governance and institutions. World Trade Report 2004.* Retrieved from http://www.wto.org/english/res_e/booksp_e/anrep_e/wtr04_2d_e.pdf

WTO. (2010). *International trade statistics 2010.* Retrieved August 16, 2014, from http://www.wto.org/english/res_e/statis_e/its2010_e/its10_toc_e.htm

WTO. (2014a). *Understanding the WTO: Organization, members and observers.* Retrieved August 11, 2014, from http://www.wto.org/english/thewto_e/whatis_e/tif_e/org6_e.htm

WTO. (2014b). *What is the WTO? About the WTO:* A statement by former Director-General Pascal Lamy. Retrieved August 10, 2014, from http://www.wto.org/english/thewto_e/whatis_e/wto_dg_stat_e.htm

Yeyati, E., Stein, E., & Daude, C. (2003). *Regional integration and the location of FDI* (Working Paper No. 492). Washington, DC: Inter-American Development Bank.

About the Authors

Nader Asgary, PhD

Nader Asgary is currently a Professor of Management and Economics at Bentley University and President of Cyrus Institute of Knowledge. He has taught courses in International Business, International Economics, International Management Behavior, Economics, Economic Development, Econometrics, and Finance at the undergraduate and graduate levels for more than 20 years, and he has been the recipient of many educator awards and grants. Dr. Asgary has published in numerous national and international journals, such as Economic Inquiry and Journal of Business Ethics, has participated in many international and national conference presentations and has been a guest speaker and professional journal reviewer. He was named Associate Provost for International Relations and Director of the Cronin International Centre (CIC) in 2006. As Associate Provost, he manages all things "international" at Bentley, and led many initiatives to enhance the globalization agenda of the University. Dr. Asgary studied at Texas A&M University, where he received a BS in Civil Engineering, and then worked in the public and private sector in Middle East for several years. He received his MA and PhD in economics at the University of Houston and has taught at State University of New York and Bentley University.

Dinorah Frutos-Bencze, PhD

Dr. Frutos-Bencze is an Assistant Professor of International Business at Saint Anselm College in Manchester, NH. Dr. Frutos-Bencze has over 9 years of

Foundations of Global Business, pages 169–171
Copyright © 2015 by Information Age Publishing
169

professional experience as Human Resources Manager and Training and Development Manager in Europe and the United States. From 1996 to 2005, Dr. Frutos held various positions in the HR field at Euronet Worldwide Inc. In addition to corporate experience, Dr. Frutos-Bencze was the Associate Dean of Online Business Programs at Southern New Hampshire University-COCE where she supervised over 75 adjunct faculty each term. Additional responsibilities included ensuring academic integrity of curriculum content and developing business programs.

Dr. Frutos-Bencze has published several peer reviewed articles and chapters in journals such as the *International Trade Journal* and *IGI-Global*. Her most recent research has been about economic integration (specifically the CAFTA region), applications of system dynamics modeling to international business, as well as exploring the impacts of international business on environmental sustainability. Dr. Frutos-Bencze is fluent in English, Spanish, and Czech. Dr. Frutos-Bencze received her MS in Chemistry at the University of New Mexico, MBA at Oxford Brookes, England, and her PhD in International Business at Southern New Hampshire University.

Massood V. Samii, PhD

Massood Samii is professor of International Business and the director of the Institute for International Business at Southern New Hampshire University. Previously he was the chair of the department and director of Ph.D. program. He was also senior lecturer on Construction finance at MIT's Department of Civil and Environmental Engineering from 1992 to 2007. Formerly, he was with the Kennedy School of Government at Harvard University, where he did research on global energy and oil markets. He served OPEC Secretariat in Vienna Austria between 1979 and 1987 as a senior economist and the head of the finance section. During his tenure at OPEC, he was involved in a numerous projects including OPEC Long Term Strategy, and Oil Pricing Strategy.

Dr. Samii has directed numerous projects for the U.S. Department of Education. In 2004, he was recognized by the Governor of State of New Hampshire and the New Hampshire International Trade Association (NHITA) for outstanding contribution to the State's International Business and Trade. He was a member of the Advisory Board of Governor Office of International Commerce (OIC) and of the Texas A&M International University PhD program. In addition, he has done numerous executive training and consulting internationally. He was on editorial board of *Journal of Emerging Markets*, and the *International Trade Journal*.

Dr. Samii has lectured and published widely on issues of energy, economic development, risk analysis, and international business. His articles have appeared in the journals of *Energy Policy, Energy and Development, OPEC Review, Petroleum Management*, the *International Trade Journal*, and *Thunderbird International Business*. He was an official observer representative to the IMF Interim Committee, World Bank Development Committee, and UNCTAD Trade and Development Committee. His book titled *International Business and Information Technology* was published by Routledge. His area of research includes risk analysis and management for foreign direct investment, international business strategy, dynamic strategy, and international oil market.

Printed in the United States
By Bookmasters